The Wisdom of
ELEANOR ROOSEVELT

The Wisdom of
ELEANOR ROOSEVELT

EDITED BY
DONALD WIGAL, PH.D.

PHILOSOPHICAL
LIBRARY

B Roosevelt

 CITADEL PRESS
Kensington Publishing Corp.
www.kensingtonbooks.com

CITADEL PRESS BOOKS are published by

Kensington Publishing Corp.
850 Third Avenue
New York, NY 10022

All Kensington titles, imprints, and distributed lines are available at special quantity discounts for bulk purchases for sales promotions, premiums, fund-raising, educational, or institutional use. Special book excerpts or customized printings can also be created to fit specific needs. For details, write or phone the office of the Kensington special sales manager: Kensington Publishing Corp., 850 Third Avenue, New York, NY 10022, attn: Special Sales Department; phone 1-800-221-2647.

First printing: June 2003

10 9 8 7 6 5 4 3 2 1

Printed in the United States of America

Library of Congress Control Number: 2002113396

ISBN 0-8065-2478-2

Please do not imagine that I am planning to give you advice that will eventually solve all your problems. We all know that no human being is infallible . . . I am not setting myself up as an oracle. But it may be that in the varied life I have had there have been certain experiences which other people will find useful.

—Mrs. Eleanor Roosevelt

CONTENTS

INTRODUCTION

Few people in history have reacted to their times and at the same time influenced them more than did Anna Eleanor Roosevelt (1884–1962). Not only did she live during the most turbulent years of the twentieth century, but she also was often uniquely at the very pulse-taking points of its events.

Mrs. Roosevelt, heroine and humanitarian, advocate and activist, prolific writer and leader, is justly considered one of the most influential women of the twentieth century. She was chosen the most admired American by a Gallup poll in 1958. No future reckoning or reassessment of history is likely to remove that remarkable distinction from her. However, interestingly, she is not one of the most frequently quoted people of her century, in spite of her hundreds of newspaper columns and articles, four autobiographical volumes, several other published books, many speeches and interviews, and volumes of letters.

There might be as many famous quotations *about* Mrs. Roosevelt as there are quotations *by* her. The most famous might be Harry S. Truman's dedication of her as "First Lady of the World." Her friend, Adlai Stevenson, stated: "Certainly one of God's noblest, strongest creations was Eleanor Roosevelt." Another friend, the novelist Martha Gellhorn, states that "there has been no other woman of her stature in pubic life and probably there never will be again." She was also named "Woman of the Century" by the National Women's Hall of Fame. Psychologist Howard Gardner noted that both she and Martin Luther King Jr. were "leaders of non-dominant groups . . . leaders of the dispossessed." In her *Leadership the Eleanor Roosevelt Way*, Robin Gerber adds that "Eleanor led by breaking down isolation, by bringing communities together and forging ties across racial and class lines."

When she was first lady of New York State and later first lady of the United States, there were several other leaders with even greater platforms. Her own husband, of course, was most notable among the giants with whom she often shared ideas. This was at a time when few women had spoken out about anything, let alone on key issues of their day. In the 1950s she represented her country in travels to England, France, India, Japan, and the Soviet Union. The queen of England, Winston Churchill, Gandhi, and other giants of history shared with her more than merely social conversations. She gave to them of her wisdom, and passed on to us theirs as well. She was indeed an admirable reservoir as well as an exceptionally effective channel of information, knowledge, opinion, advice, wit, and inspiration.

Mrs. Roosevelt

During her lifetime, even those close to the first lady referred to her as "Mrs. Roosevelt," rarely as "Eleanor." We here respect that practice even at the risk of being repetitious. We feel it is a small price to pay for using each opportunity we have to show respect for our distinguished subject.

Quotations

This book presents nearly five hundred excerpts from her works, indexed by many major concepts and key words. There are only a few quotations from Mrs. Roosevelt's many writings found in the most popular collections of quotations. For instance, there are only two in John Bartlett's

Familiar Quotations (16th Edition). Some collections in fact do not quote her at all, but all of the more famous quotes are included here. A fine compendium of quotations edited by Alex Ayres titled *The Wit and Wisdom of Eleanor Roosevelt* (Meridian, 1996) demonstrates that one need not call on many of the available resources to find a surplus of brilliant passages from Mrs. Roosevelt. But, Ayres's book is not focused on our theme of wisdom.

The quotations are presented in general chronological order by year, with highlights of Mrs. Roosevelt's life and current events. Events mentioned within a given year might not be in strict chronology.

Letters

Unlike most previous collections of excerpts from the writings of Mrs. Roosevelt, this one includes numerous quotations from her published personal letters. Specifically, included are passages from her letters to her daughter, Anna (as quoted also in *Mother and Daughter*, by Bernard Asbell), and to her husband's successor in the White House, Harry S. Truman, as quoted also in *Eleanor and Harry*, by Steve Neal. Also included are excerpts from her letter to her friend David Gurewitsch as quoted also in his widow Edna P. Gurewitsch's *Kindred Souls*. Finally, there are excerpts from letters to her friend Lorena Hickok as quoted in *Empty Without You*, by Rodger Streitmatter.

Of her intimate letters, we have not included those excerpts, typically taken out of context, that seem to be of interest only to the merely curious or to only superficial journalism. Rather, we have sought out the pearls of wisdom that can travel beyond personal feelings to more universal applications or understandings.

Mrs. Roosevelt stressed to President Truman that she "would not use a private letter in a public way at any time" (May 5, 1945, *Eleanor and Harry*). We respectfully propose that our intention here is to share her wisdom with the world, not invade privacy in any way.

Writing Style

As Mrs. Roosevelt admitted to President Truman, her handwriting was "anything but legible" (May 5, 1945, *Eleanor and Harry*). That might account for some of the difficulties in transcribing the letters. But it is her style that might distract the reader even after transcription.

Readers of the letters of Mrs. Roosevelt often mention that her informal writing style presents problems. Among the distinctive habits of the writer is her frequent use of the ampersand (&), especially between sentences, creating run-on sentences. The sentences of an entire letter might all be linked with ampersands. Rather than be distracting, these linked sentences can remind the reader of the very active mind behind even the most casual of comments. While probably not to be advocated in writing courses, her style reminds us that she was continually making associations between one idea and another, even when the two seem to us at first unrelated.

The editor's temptation is to "correct" the writing style. However, we have here been faithful to the published editions of these letters, with a minimum of editing where the slips are obvious (e.g., changing *effect* for *affect*, *insure* for *ensure*). Nearly all of the letters quoted here are informal, and were obviously never intended to be published.

Time Capsules

Many excerpts from the writings of Eleanor Roosevelt stand on their own without knowing more specifically where or when they were said. However, knowing to whom Mrs. Roosevelt is speaking often helps the reader appreciate passages from letters, for example. In fact, when seen in the context of their times and places, many of her comments can be more appreciated. Her statement, for instance, that "Mr. (Richard M.) Nixon never has anything but hindsight," can be appreciated more fully when we see that she said that in 1960, before John F. Kennedy defeated Nixon to win the presidency later that year.

At the beginning of each set of quotations for each decade, we present dates and highlights from the life of Mrs. Roosevelt and related or significant contemporary events are presented. Some of these facts are based on materials provided by the Franklin D. Roosevelt Library, Hyde Park, and other authoritative sources. (Cf. "Eleanor Roosevelt: Time Line," *My Day*, edited by David Emblidge.) Our chronology of her many writings is as in *Courage in a Dangerous World: The Political Writings of Eleanor Roosevelt*, edited by Allida M. Black. Concerning the ordering of historical events, we considered the definitive biographer of our subject to be Joseph Lash, as seen in his *Eleanor and Franklin, 1971.*

Other such concise outlines of a celebrity life typically include titles of books written by the subject. Ours also seeks to list some of what influenced our subject by noting *what* she read. Specifically, we note in our time lines several of over fifty introductions or forewords to books that Mrs. Roosevelt wrote.

While in these time capsules historical facts are mentioned in their correct years, the events noted within each year might not be in strict chronological order. Moreover, the writings of Mrs. Roosevelt are typically noted here as "written" in the year the work was published, whereas her actual writing may have been done in previous years. At least five articles and two book introductions by Mrs. Roosevelt were published the year after her death.

"My Day"

The newspaper columns of Eleanor Roosevelt were titled "My Day," which began in 1936 and continued faithfully to the year of her death, 1962. The columns appeared in the *New York Post* (1957–1962), as well as in many major newspapers, including the *New York Herald Tribune*, the *Milwaukee Journal*, the *Kansas City Star*, and the *Atlanta Constitution*. These are quoted here more often than any other source. However, excerpts alone would not capture the style and spirit of these essays. Therefore, to help the reader appreciate how Mrs. Roosevelt developed her ideas, twenty-seven complete columns, from 1939–1962, are appended here to the quotations.

The United Nations and Human Rights

On reading the Universal Declaration of Human Rights in Braille, Helen Keller stated: "My soul stood erect, exultant, envisioning a new world where the light of justice for every individual will be unclouded."

While Mrs. Roosevelt was not the sole author of The Universal Declaration of Human Rights, she is acknowledged to have been its principal driving force. In fact, all of the key notions of the declaration might be found as the-

matic to her lifelong convictions expressed, albeit often in-
formally, in her books, articles, letters, speeches, and interviews. She wrote several articles and the introductions to
two books that commented on the declaration.

On December 10, 1948, the General Assembly of the United
Nations adopted and proclaimed the Universal Declaration
of Human Rights, the full text of which appears at the end
of the book, as it does in several of the books that have been
written about Mrs. Roosevelt.

Following that historic act, the Assembly called upon all
member countries to publicize the text of the Declaration
and "to cause it to be disseminated, displayed, read and ex-
pounded principally in schools and other educational insti-
tutions, without distinction based on the political status of
countries or territories."

The European spelling of certain words in the charter
(*color* as *colour, honor* as *honour,* etc.) were changed here to
standard American spellings.

Index

The listing of topics and key concepts found in the quotations is given at the end of this collection. Following a certain theme throughout the excerpts, the reader might notice
a certain evolution of her thoughts, obviously influenced by
the times and experience.

Wisdom

Mrs. Roosevelt often called on wisdom as the most important element in a decision-making process. A typical passage
is seen in a letter to President Harry S. Truman in which she

asks the president to join several other notable people in signing a position statement. She stated that she was hoping that he might sign it "if you think it is a wise move at this time. If there are any changes which you think wise, we would of course want you to make them. If you don't think it wise, you must, of course, also let me know" (January 13, 1956, *Eleanor and Harry*).

Years before, one morning shortly after the end of World War II, Mrs. Roosevelt wrote to President Truman after he had called her the night before. Her comment to him is surely thematic to all the advice she gave not only to heads of state during her life, but to us as well as we call on her insights: "You will have pressures from every side. I am sure your own wisdom and experience and faith in God will guide you aright" (August 15, 1945, *Eleanor and Harry*).

ACKNOWLEDGMENTS

For her reply to our requests, I am pleased to thank Nancy Roosevelt Ireland, Trustee, Anna E. Roosevelt Trust. Also, the FDR and Truman Presidential Libraries, editor Richard Ember, Kelly Archer for help with permissions, Stephany Evans for heroic patience as my agent, William Kuhns for sharing his library and advice, Sherry Mahady and Paola Montoya for research, and especially for Catherine O'Reilly for her dedication and meticulous attention to detail, and George Sullivan for advice.

I dedicate my work here to the hundreds of colleagues in Common Bond (a fraternity of former priests and religious men and women), who understood my need to retreat from my service to them in order to complete this other labor of love.

I am sure they all join with me in hopes that all readers find wisdom from Mrs. Roosevelt's extensive experience, and inspiration from her leadership, the consequences of which influenced not only her own century and her own country, but surely all the world for centuries to come.

SOURCES

While many resources were consulted, not all were sources of quotations presented in this book. Requests for reprint permission were made during August and September 2002, to the copyright holders of materials quoted herein. Only the words of Mrs. Roosevelt were quoted from these sources, unless otherwise noted.

Books by Mrs. Roosevelt

The Autobiography of Eleanor Roosevelt. Harper & Brothers, 1958 and 1978.

Christmas Book. Dodd, 1963.

Eleanor Roosevelt's Book of Common Sense Etiquette. The Macmillan Company, 1962.

Eleanor Roosevelt's "My Day": Her Acclaimed Columns. Pharos Books, 1989–91.

If You Ask Me. Appleton, 1946.

India and the Awakening East. Harper & Brothers, 1953.

It's Up to the Women. Frederick A. Stokes, 1933.

On My Own. Harper & Brothers, 1958.

Partners: The United Nations and Youth. Doubleday, 1950.

This I Remember. Harper & Brothers, 1949.

This Is My Story. Harper & Brothers, 1937.

Tomorrow Is Now. Harper & Row, 1963.

UN: Today and Tomorrow. Harper & Brothers, 1953.

You Learn by Living. Harper & Brothers, 1960.

Your Teens and Mine. Doubleday, 1961.

Letters

Eleanor and Harry: The Correspondence of Eleanor Roosevelt and Harry S. Truman. Edited by Steve Neal. Lisa Drew/Scribner, 2002.

Hunting Big Game in the Eighties: The Letters of Elliott Roosevelt, Sportsman. Charles Scribner's Sons, 1933.

Kindred Souls: The Friendship of Eleanor Roosevelt and David Gurewitsch. Edna P. Gurewitsch. St. Martin's Press, 2002.

Mother and Daughter: The Letters of Eleanor and Anna Roosevelt. (Bernard Aspbell, ed.) Coward, McCann and Geoghegan, 1982.

Empty Without You: The Intimate Letters of Eleanor Roosevelt and Lorena Kickok. Edited by Rodger Streitmatter. The Free Press, 1998.

Articles

Some writings by Mrs. Roosevelt quoted here are from magazines and books not by or about her. All citations also appear in "A Comprehensive Bibliography of the Articles of Eleanor Roosevelt," in *Courage In a Dangerous World: The Political Writings of Eleanor Roosevelt*. See "Books About Mrs. Roosevelt" below.

"Are We Overlooking the Pursuit of Happiness?" *Parents' Magazine* [Vol. 11] (September, 1936): 21, 67.

"Because the War Idea Is Obsolete," *Why Wars Must Cease*. Editor: Rose Young. New York: Macmillan, 1935, 20–29.

"First Lady Pleads for Old Age Pensions," *Social Security* [Vol. 8] (February, 1945): 3–4.

"I Want You to Write to Me," *Woman's Home Companion* (August, 1933): 4.

"Insuring Democracy," *Collier's* [Vol. 105] (June 15, 1940): 87–88.

"In Defense of Curiosity," *Saturday Evening Post* [Vol. 208] (August 24, 1935): 8–9, 64–66.

"The Moral Basis of Democracy," Howell, Soskin and Company, 1940.

"The Negro and Social Change." *Opportunity* (January, 1936): 22–23.

"The New Government Interest in the Arts," *American Magazine of Art* [Vol. 27] (September, 1934): 47.

"Women in Politics." *Woman's Press* (Y.M.C.A.) (April, 1940): 165.

Books About Mrs. Roosevelt

Leadership the Eleanor Roosevelt Way. Robin Gerber. Prentice Hall, 2002.

Courage in a Political World: The Political Writings of Eleanor Roosevelt. (Alllida M. Black, ed.) Columbia University Press, 1999. Note especially "A Comprehensive Bibliography of the Articles of Eleanor Roosevelt," an Appendix.

Eleanor and Franklin. Joseph Lash. Norton, 1971.

1884–1939

Time Line

1884 Anna Eleanor Roosevelt born, October 11.

1886 At age two, Eleanor meets her fifth cousin, Franklin Delano Roosevelt, for the first time.

1899–1902 Eleanor Roosevelt attends Allenswood School.

1901–1909 Theodore Roosevelt, Eleanor's uncle, is president of the United States.

1902 Eleanor Roosevelt makes her formal debut into New York society.

1903 Fifth cousin, Franklin Delano Roosevelt (FDR) asks Eleaanor to marry him.

1903–1904 Eleanor Roosevelt teaches calisthenics and dancing to immigrants in slum areas; investigates working conditions of laborers; joins the Consumers' League.

1904 FDR graduates from Harvard.

1905 Eleanor Roosevelt marries FDR.

1906 First child born, Anna Eleanor (d. 1975).

1907 First son born, James.

1909 Second son born and died, Franklin Delano.

1910 FDR is nominated to run for the New York Senate. He

wins campaign in traditionally Republican territory of Dutchess County.

1910 Third son born, Elliot.

1912 Mrs. Eleanor Roosevelt attends a Democratic party convention for the first time.

1913 FDR campaigns for Woodrow Wilson, who later appoints him assistant secretary of the navy, which he remains till 1920.

1914 Fourth son born, Franklin Delano Roosevelt III.

1915 Theodore Roosevelt publishes *America and the World War.*

1916 Fifth son born, John Aspinwall Roosevelt.

1918 Mrs. Roosevelt discovers her husband's affair with Lucy Mercer, her social secretary.

1918 Mrs. Roosevelt works with the navy department and the Red Cross to help World War I servicemen.

1919 Theodore Roosevelt dies.

1920 Mrs. Roosevelt supports the suffrage movement. She also joins and delivers public speeches for the League of Women Voters.

1921 FDR discovers he has poliomyelitis. Mrs. Roosevelt takes care of him and encourages him to return to politics. She writes "Common Sense Versus Party Regularity" for the League of Women Voters of New York State.

1922 Mrs. Eleanor Roosevelt joins the Women's Trade Union League and The Women's Division of the Democratic State Committee.

1923 Mrs. Roosevelt writes "Why I Am a Democrat" for the Junior League Bulletin.

1924 FDR learns how to use crutches and braces in order to appear in public as merely lame, not paraplegic. He gives his "Happy Warrior" speech as part of the nomination of New York Governor Alfred E. Smith for president. Mrs. Roosevelt writes "How to Interest Women in Voting" for the Women's Democratic Campaign Manual. She began to frequently make what she called "occasional speeches."

1925 Mrs. Roosevelt and two friends launch a furniture factory at the Val-Kill cottage in Hyde Park, New York.

1927 Mrs. Eleanor Roosevelt begins to teach at the Todhunter School. She studies black issues and befriends Mary McLeod Bethune, president of Bethune-Cookman College.

1928 FDR publishes *The Happy Warrior: Alfred E. Smith.* He is elected governor of New York. Mrs. Roosevelt is named the director of the Bureau of Women's Activities of the Democratic National Convention. She writes "Women Must Learn to Play the Game as Men Do" for *Red Book* magazine.

1930 Mrs. Roosevelt writes the introduction to the biography of Margaret Fuller by Margaret Bell. She also writes ten periodic reports titled "A Summer Trip Abroad," for the Women's Democratic News.

1931 After deciding to run for president, FDR does not tell his wife for some time. She later reveals "From the personal standpoint, I did not want my husband to be president. . . . I never mentioned my feelings on the subject to him."

1932 Mrs. Roosevelt writes the introduction to the National Home Library Foundation edition of works by Lewis Carroll, including *Alice's Adventures in Wonderland.*

1933 FDR is elected president of the United States. Mrs. Roosevelt later writes: "I had watched Mrs. Theodore Roosevelt and had seen what it meant to be the wife of a president, and I cannot say I was pleased at the prospect." Mrs. Roosevelt becomes the first first lady to hold press conferences. She helps establish an experimental homestead project for coal miners in West Virginia. The nation's banking system collapses. Approximately 14 million Americans are unemployed. FDR delivers a speech stating, "the only thing we have to fear, is fear itself." FDR will be reelected three times.

1934 Mrs. Roosevelt helps initiate the National Youth Administration. She arranges for discussions between black leaders and the president concerning the need for anti-lynching legislation. She writes the introduction to James Howard's *Getting Acquainted with Your Children*.

1935 Mrs. Roosevelt begins writing "My Day," the syndicated column that she continues writing for the rest of her life. She would average about five hundred words a day, six days a week, for twenty-six years.

1937 *Colonial Policies of the United States*, by Theodore Roosevelt published. While writing the first book of her autobiography, "This Is My Story," she burns FDR's letters to her (her letters to him, however, were preserved by FDR). Ten installments of the autobiography appear in *Ladies' Home Journal*. She also writes the introduction to *The White House: An Informal History*, by Ethel Lewis.

1939 Mrs. Eleanor Roosevelt defies Alabama segregation laws by sitting with blacks at the Southern Conference for Human Welfare. Listening to Hitler's speech to the Reichstag on the radio, Mrs. Roosevelt mentions that she knows "enough German" to understand the speech did not mention God.

1939–1940 Mrs. Roosevelt helps relocate European labor and socialist deputies and families.

Quotations

1. It depends on what each of us does, what we consider democracy means, and what we consider freedom in a democracy means and whether we really care about it enough to face ourselves and our prejudices and to make up our minds what we really want our nation to be, and what its relationship is to be to the rest of the world.
August 1933, "I Want You to Write to Me."

2. Please do not imagine that I am planning to give you advice that will eventually solve all your problems. We all know that no human being is infallible, and [. . .] I am not setting myself up as an oracle. But it may be that in the varied life I have had there have been certain experiences which other people will find useful [. . .].
August 1933, "I Want You to Write to Me."

3. [To Lorena] Dear one, & so you think they gossip about us. Well they must at least think we stand separation rather well! I am always so much more optimistic than you are. I suppose because I care so little what "they" say!
November 27, 1933, Empty Without You.

4. [To Lorena] I had a funny letter to-day. A woman said she read all I wrote on child labor & she had had 13 [children] & wouldn't I please tell her how to stop it!
December 5, 1933, Empty Without You.

5. [To Lorena] The [Albert] Einsteins arrived [at the White House] & are priceless, so German & so simple with many wise gentle German qualities.
January 24, 1934, Empty Without You.

6. [To Lorena] People are never satisfied [. . .] unless things are done for them. It is unfortunate that we have to do it, they like doing for themselves. Human beings are poor things, think how much discipline we need ourselves & don't get too discouraged.
January 29, 1934, Empty Without You.

7. Old people love their own things even more than young people do. It means so much to sit in the same old chair you sat in for a great many years, to see the same pictures that you always looked at!
February 1934, "First Lady Pleads for Old Age Pensions."

8. Dearest [Lorena], we are happy to-gether & strong rela- tionships have to grow deep roots. We're growing them now, partly because we are separated, the foliage & the flowers will come somehow I'm sure of it. [. . .] Love is a queer thing, it hurts but it gives one so much more in return!
February 4, 1934, Empty Without You.

9. That is the great power of the artist, the power to make people hear and understand, through music and literature, or to paint something which we ordinary people feel but cannot reveal. That great gift is something which, if it is rec- ognized, if it is given the support and the help and the recognition from people as a whole throughout this coun- try, is going to mean an enormous amount in our develop- ment as a people.
November 1934, "The New Governmental Interest in the Arts."

10 . I hope that in every community throughout this coun- try, that spirit can be fostered which makes a piece of work worthwhile because you love to do it, regardless of the time you put into it, and because it is worth everything

that you can put into it to give to the world a really perfect thing.

November 1934, "The New Governmental Interest in the Arts."

11. [To Anna] I'm an idiotic puritan & I wish I had the right kind of sense of humor & could enjoy certain things. At least, thank God, none of you children have inherited that streak in me, it is as well to have some of Father's ease & balance in these things! . . .

November 19, 1934, Mother and Daughter.

12. History records many bloody battles which were fought for no better reason than it was impossible to communicate with the combatants and tell them the war was over.

1935, "Because the War Idea Is Obsolete."

13. People are prone to say that history repeats itself and that today in the United States they can see the period of Roman decadence, if not actually repeating itself, at least drawing nearer and nearer. They are prone to say, too, that Greece and Rome were conquered by barbarians because they ceased to be able to fight. I doubt if these countries were conquered simply because they ceased to be as war-like as the barbarian. I think they were conquered because they ceased to be a forward-moving civilization. They had the opportunity and they failed. They came to a point where they declined physically, mentally and morally. It was not only that they could not fight from a physical standpoint, they were worthless and gradually decaying from every point of view.

1935, "Because the War Idea Is Obsolete."

14. If we are to do away with the war idea, one of the first steps will be to do away with all possibility of private

profit. It does not matter very much which side you fight on in any war. The effects are just the same whether you win or whether you lose.

1935, "Because the War Idea Is Obsolete."

15. The easy answer to it all is that human nature is such that we cannot do away with war. That seems to me like saying that human nature is so made that we must destroy ourselves. After all, human nature has some intelligence and the world's experience has already proved that there are ways in which disputes can be settled if people have intelligence and show good will toward one another. To do this on a national scale, as it is done the individual, people must first be convinced that the war idea is obsolete. When people become convinced of this they will convince their governments and the governments will find the way to stop war.

1935, "Because the War Idea Is Obsolete."

16. [To Lorena] I love other people in the same way or differently but each one has their place & one cannot compare them. I do know for myself that if I know someone I love is unhappy I can't be happy & I would be happier to see or to know they were happy even if [it] meant giving up my own relationship to them in whole or in part. I'd probably hope to get back enriched someday but if not, well, I know no one I love I wouldn't rather see happy & I hope they wouldn't worry about my hurt because it would be so much less than watching them hurt. I don't think I'd run away either, unless they wanted me to!

May 13, 1935, Empty Without You.

17. It is not always our own fault when we lack curiosity, for our environment may have prevented its development. The

lack of curiosity in parents will often mean that they will try to eliminate it in their children, and thus keep their homes from stimulating the youthful urge to acquire knowledge.

August 24, 1935, "In Defense of Curiosity."

18. The great experiences of life are the same wherever you live and whether you are rich or poor. Birth and death, courage and cowardice, kindness and cruelty, love and hate, are no respecters of persons, and they are the occasions and emotions which bring about most of the experience of life. You cannot prevent unhappiness or sorrow entering into any life—even the fairy godmother of the legend could not give freedom from these experiences—but curiosity will ensure an ever-recurring interest in life and will give you the needed impetus to turn your most baleful experience to some kind of good service.

August 24, 1935, "In Defense of Curiosity."

19. I often wonder, as I look at the stars at night, if someday we will find a way to communicate and travel from one to the other. . . . Perhaps the day will come when our curiosity will not only carry us out of our home and out of ourselves to a better understanding of material things, but will make us able to understand one another and to know what the Lord meant when He said, "He that hath ears to hear, let him hear." And we might well add: "He that hath eyes to see, let him see."

August 24, 1935, "In Defense of Curiosity."
Cf. Lamentations 5:21, and Matthew 11:15.

20. There is no reason why all of the races in this country should not live together each of them giving from their particular gift something to the other, and contributing an ex-

ample to the world of "peace on earth, good will toward men."
August 24, 1935, "In Defense of Curiosity." Cf. Luke 2:14.

21. [To Lorena] You need not have been afraid that your criticism would discourage me, you see I haven't the feeling that the things [I write] are good in themselves. I've always felt it was largely [the Roosevelt] name [they wanted][. . .] If I can't do this after giving it a good try then I must do something else that is all & one can only find out by trying.
September 5, 1935, Empty Without You.

22. [To Lorena] Darling, don't let anyone hold memorial meetings for me after I leave you. It is cruel to those who really love you & miss you & means nothing to the others except an obligation fulfilled & certainly it can mean nothing to the spirit in another sphere if it is there at all! I'd like to be remembered happily if that is possible, if that can't be then I'd rather be forgotten.
December 19, 1935, Empty Without You.

23. No one can make you feel inferior without your consent.
1936, This Is My Story.

24. We have long held in this country that ability should be the criterion on which all people are judged. It seems to me that we must come to recognize this criterion in dealing with all human beings, and not place any limitations upon their achievements except such as may be imposed by their own character and intelligence.
January 1936, "The Negro and Social Change."

25. There is [. . .] one consolation to anyone who lives in the public eye, namely, that while it may be most difficult to keep the world from knowing where you dine and what

you eat and what you wear, so much interest is focused on these somewhat unimportant things that you are really left completely free to live your own inner life as you wish.
January 7, 1936, "My Day."

26. Thank God, few people are so poor that they do not have an inner life which feeds the real springs of thought and action. So, if I may offer a thought in consolation to others who for a time have to live in a "goldfish bowl," it is: "Don't worry because people know all that you do, for the really important things about anyone are what they are and what they think and feel, and the more you live in a 'goldfish bowl' the less people really know about you!"
January 7, 1936, "My Day."

27. With the new day comes new strength and new thoughts.
January 8, 1936, "My Day."

28. We must equalize educational opportunities throughout the country. We must see that rural children have as good a general education as city children can acquire, and the advantages of both groups must if possible be made interchangeable. No city child should grow up without knowing the beauty of spring in the country or where milk comes from, how vegetables grow and what it is like to play in a field instead of on a city street. No country child who knows these things should be deprived, however, of museums, books, music, and better teachers because it is easier to find them and to pay for them in big cities than it is in rural districts.
March 1936, "Are We Overlooking the Pursuit of Happiness?"

29. Real prosperity can only come out when everybody prospers.
March 19, 1936, "My Day."

30. Even if it cost a little more to employ more people for a time, in the end we will all be more prosperous as the buying power of the nation is restored.
March 19, 1936, "My Day."

31. As I [. . .] looked at the people who in spite of their handicap were doing so much, I could not help but think of what an obligation their example put on the rest of us.
March 26, 1936, "My Day."

32. A wise aunt of mine used to say: "Do anything you want to do, but always be quite sure that in your heart of hearts you are at peace with yourself about doing it. It does not matter what people think, but if you are uncomfortable yourself then you will have no happiness." I believe that I would rather like to go through life with this more cheerful philosophy of trying to make duty coincide as far as possible with what one would like to do, being sure, however, that what I do leaves my inner consciousness satisfied and untroubled.
July 13, 1936, "My Day."

33. [To Lorena] It is only when one is oneself very unhappy that one ever thinks about the individual right to the pursuit of happiness. When you reach my age, it comes less & less often [. . .]
August 3, 1936, Empty Without You.

34. Make up your mind to live as happily and as fully as you can. Seize on everything that comes your way which makes life more interesting, or agreeable.
January 1, 1937, "My Day."

35. [To Anna] Pa is both nervous & tired. [. . .] I thought

stupidly his little outburst of boredom on meals was amusing & human & used it in my column [. . .] James [FDR's servant] came & reproved me & said I must distinguish between things which were personal and should not be said or none of them would dare to talk to me & he thought I should apologize to Father. [. . .] I am grieved at my poor judgment & only hope it won't be remembered long. Will I be glad when we leave the W.H. & I can be on my own!

March 3, 1937, Mother and Daughter.

36. It would be impossible to say how often and to what extent American government processes have been turned in a new direction because of her [America's] determination. [. . .]

March 6, 1937, "My Day."

37. [. . .] as a rule women know not only what men know, but much that men will never know. For, how many men really know the heart and soul of a woman?

March 6, 1937, "My Day."

38. I know women should never discuss mathematics, our minds don't function that way. But, on the whole, [. . .] everything was so carefully explained to me and I was so persistent that I think they finally got my point of view—which was in this particular case that mathematics made little difference, though it does seem to loom very large in the masculine mind.

April 21, 1937, "My Day."

39. In coming years, I wonder if we are not going to have more respect for women who work and give work to others than for women who sit at home with many idle hours on their hands or fill their time with occupations which may indirectly provide work for others but which give them none of the satisfactions of real personal achievement.

April 21, 1937, "My Day."

40. Of course, when we talked of "the front" in connection with future wars, we are taking it for granted that future wars will be much like those of the past, whereas most people believe that future wars will have no fronts. What we hear of Spain and China makes this seem very probable. Gases and airplanes will not be directed only against armed forces, or military centers, they may be used for the breaking of morale in the opposing nation. That will mean shelling of unfortified cities, towns and villages, and the killing of women and children. In fact this means the participation in war of entire populations.

1938, "This Troubled World."

41. We can establish no real trust between nations until we acknowledge the power of love above all other power.

1938, "This Troubled World."

42. We will have to want peace, want it enough to pay for it, pay for it in our own behavior and in material ways. We will have to want it enough to overcome our lethargy and go out and find all those in other countries who want it as much as we do.

1938, "This Troubled World."

43. I often wonder as I look around the world whether any of us, even we women, really want peace. Women should realize better than anyone else, that the spirit of peace has to begin in the relationship between two individuals. They know that a child alone may be unhappy because he is alone, but there will be no quarreling until another child appears on the scene, and then the fur will fly, if each of them desires the same thing at the same time.

1938, "This Troubled World."

44. Women have watched this for generations and must know, if peace is going to come about in the world, the way to start is by getting a better understanding between individuals. From this germ a better understanding between groups of people will grow.

1938, "This Troubled World."

45. Human beings either must recognize the fact that what serves the people as a whole serves them best as individuals and, through selfish or unselfish interests, they become people of good intentions and honesty. If not we will be unable to move forward except as we have moved in the past with recourse to force, and constant, suspicious watchfulness on the part of individuals and groups towards each other. The preservation of our civilization seems to demand a permanent change of attitude and therefore every effort should be bent towards bringing about this change in human nature through education. This is a slow way and, in the meantime, we need not sit with folded hands and feel that no steps can be taken to ward off the dangers which constantly beset us.

1938, "This Troubled World."

46. Whatever work I am doing is interesting, because it is a game to find time enough to do it.

April 18, 1938, "My Day."

47. Anything repeated over and over again brings people to the point where they are stale and need a change of environment to vary their thoughts.

April 18, 1938, "My Day."

48. I'm always sorry for the man who is beaten or the team

which loses. Much effort has gone into training and preparation and it must be such a terrible letdown. I've never seen a fight and probably never shall, but every time I see a crew race or a football game, I grieve over the boys who are beaten and slump in their boats, or the team that has to go off the field cheering the victors when their hearts are filled with despair.

June 23, 1938, "My Day."

49. It is interesting to be in a position where you have the opportunity of knowing the truth about a few subjects, but it has its unfortunate side in that it makes you doubt the veracity of so many things which you read and hear.

August 8, 1938, "My Day."

50. [To Anna] I feel [. . .] that Hitler has acquired all he wanted this time and will begin again to get the next thing he wants when he is ready to do so. Therefore we have only postponed a war unless we are prepared to let Hitler and his ideas dominate Europe. It does not seem to be our business really and yet I wonder if we can remain uninfluenced by the growth of those ideas.

October 3, 1938, Mother and Daughter.

51. The greatest contribution the older generation can give, I think, to the younger generation, is the feeling that there is someone to fall back upon, more especially when the hard times of life come upon them. That is so even when we know that we have brought those hard times upon ourselves.

November 11, 1938, "My Day."

52. Having children is, perhaps, the beginning of an education for them, but it is certainly the beginning of an education for the parents

November 11, 1938, "My Day."

53. Without doubt human beings are the most interesting study in the world.

January 5, 1939, "My Day."

54. As far as possible, I never discuss questions of partisan politics, [in this column] but now and then it seems to me that public questions arise which are of particular interest to women and which far transcend any partisan lines.

February 3, 1939, "My Day."

55. [. . .] all wars eventually act as boomerangs and the victor suffers as much as the vanquished.

February 7, 1939, "My Day."

56. It takes courage to love, but pain through love is the purifying fire which those who love generously know.

April 1, 1939, "My Day."

57. Happiness may exist under all conditions, given the right kind of people and sufficient economic security for adequate food and shelter.

May 31, 1939, "My Day."

58. In the real things in life, everyone stands on the same level and God sends us disciplines in order that we may better understand the suffering of other people.

June 13, 1939, "My Day."

59. It seems to me that it is the basic right of any human being to work.

June 16, 1939, "My Day."

60. We do not dwell upon man's lower nature any more than we have to in life, but we know it exists and we pass

over it charitably and are surprised how much there is of fineness that comes out of the baser clay. Even from life's sorrows some good must come.

June 28, 1939, "My Day."

61. The woman who has trained herself has the advantage over a man in that she still has her intuition, but to it she has added his gift of examining facts and evaluating all the factors entering into a situation.

August 5, 1939, "My Day."

62. Negotiation, mediation or arbitration are just words, but any one of them if put into practice now by people who really want to keep peace, might mean life instead of death to hundreds of thousands.

August 26, 1939, "My Day."

63. [To Lorena] War must affect us all but there is no use in making people fear our being drawn in till it is necessary & I pray that may never be.

September 3, 1939, Empty Without You.

64. [To Lorena] [. . .] questions [being asked by people attending the lectures] are dull, run about like this: "Do you think we can keep out of war? What do women do to keep us out of war? What can we do to remain neutral?" Last night I had written questions & was asked if I loved my husband, which I did not answer!

September 23, 1939, Empty Without You.

65. Real loving means work, thinking of each other day in and day out, unselfishness, and effort to understand the growth of the soul and mind of the other individual, and to adjust and complement that other person day by day.

October 20, 1939, "My Day."

66. Keeping up romance, keeping up constant interest in each other by a meticulous care for the little things which were important when you were in love, this is all a part of loving.

October 20, 1939, "My Day."

67. No writing has any real value which is not the expression of genuine thought and feeling.

December 20, 1939, "My Day."

1940–1949

Time Line

1940 Mrs. Roosevelt writes the introductions to three books about American youth, as well as over thirty magazine articles on a wide range of topics, including three for *Good Housekeeping* magazine on "Women in Politics."

1941 Pearl Harbor is attacked by Japan. The U.S. enters World War II. The war continues till 1945. FDR's mother dies. A few weeks later Mrs. Roosevelt's brother dies. She notes "it was like losing a child."

1941–1944 Mrs. Roosevelt serves as Assistant Director of Civilian Defense with New York City Mayor Fiorello LaGuardia.

1942 Mrs. Roosevelt reviews *The American Presidency* by Harold Laski for the *Harvard Law Review.*

1943 To boost military troop morale, Mrs. Roosevelt secretly travels to military bases in the South Pacific.

1944 Mrs. Roosevelt writes the foreword to *Women in the Postwar World* for the *Journal of Educational Sociology.*

1945 Ms. Roosevelt joins the NAACP. While at a benefit, Mrs. Roosevelt is called and asked to come home at once. She senses correctly that FDR has died. "Somehow in emergencies one moves automatically," she later notes. She personally informs Vice President Harry Truman.

1945 President Truman asks Mrs. Roosevelt to be a U.S. delegate to the United Nations, a responsibility which she kept till 1952, and again from 1961 to 1962. Her nomination is confirmed by the Senate. "I accepted in fear and trembling," she later recalls. She writes the introduction to the *White House Conference on Rural Education*. She works to open the ranks of the Army Nurse Corps to black women.

1946 Mrs. Roosevelt writes the foreword to her son Elliott's recollections of FDR in *As He Saw It*. (See 1948 for a related foreword.)

1947 Mrs. Roosevelt is elected chairperson of the United National Human Rights Commission. She begins drafting the Declaration of Human Rights. She initiates a drive to create Americans for Democratic Action.

1948 Mrs. Roosevelt manages to get the United Nations General Assembly to approve the Universal Declaration of Human Rights. She writes the foreword to *F.D.R.: His Personal Letters*, edited by her son Elliott and James Rosenau. A second volume, also with an introduction by Mrs. Roosevelt, will appear in 1950.

1949 Mrs. Roosevelt's *This I Remember* is published in seven installments in *McCall's Magazine*. She writes the introduction to *Freedom's Character: The Universal Declaration of Human Rights* by O. Frederick Nolde. Also, she writes the foreword to *Mark Twain and F.D.R.* by Cyril Clemens.

Quotations

68. [. . .] I am hoping in this little book to be able to give a clearer definition of the thinking of one citizen in a Democracy. By so doing it may be possible to stimulate the thoughts of many people so that they will force themselves to decide what Democracy means to them—whether they

can believe in it as fervently as they can in their personal religion; whether it is worth a sacrifice to them, and what they consider that sacrifice must be.

1940, "The Moral Basis of Democracy."

69. Leaders of religious thought have tried for generations to make us understand that religion is a way of life which develops the spirit. Perhaps, because of the circumstances which face us today, the youth of this generation may make this type of religion a reality. I think they might thus develop for the future of this country and of the world a conception of success which will change our whole attitude toward life and civilization.

1940, "The Moral Basis of Democracy."

70. The citizens of Democracy must model themselves on the best and most unselfish life we have known in history. They may not all believe in Christ's divinity, though many will; but His life is important simply because it becomes a shining beacon of what success means. If we once establish this human standard as a measure of success, the future of Democracy is secure.

1940, "The Moral Basis of Democracy."

71. If human beings can be changed to fit a Nazi or Fascist pattern or a Communist pattern, certainly we should not lose heart at the thought of changing human nature to fit a democratic way of life. [...]

1940, "The Moral Basis of Democracy."

72. Each man may have his own religion; the church is merely the outward and visible symbol of the longing of the human soul for something to which he can aspire and which he desires beyond his own strength to achieve. If human beings can be trained for cruelty and greed and a belief in

power which comes through hate and fear and forces, certainly we can train equally well for gentleness and mercy and the power of love which come because of the strength of the good qualities to be found in the soul of every individual human being.

1940, "The Moral Basis of Democracy."

73. We live under a Democracy, under a form of government which above all other forms should make us conscious of the need we all have for this spiritual moral awakening.

1940, "The Moral Basis of Democracy."

74. Real Democracy cannot be stable and it cannot go forward to its fullest development and growth if this type of individual responsibility does not exist, not only in the leaders but in the people as a whole.

1940, "The Moral Basis of Democracy."

75. Perhaps the greatest sacrifice of all is the necessity which Democracy imposes on every individual to make himself decide in what he believes.

1940, "The Moral Basis of Democracy."

76. Our neighbors, of course, do not include only the people whom we know; they include, also, all those who live anywhere within the range of our knowledge.

1940, "The Moral Basis of Democracy."

77. We cannot remove sorrow and disappointment from the lives of human beings, but we can give them an opportunity to free themselves from mass restrictions made by man. There is nothing more exciting in the world than to be conscious of inwardly achieving something new; and anyone

who puts into practice the life of Christ on earth, cannot fail to feel the growth in his own mastery over self.

1940, "The Moral Basis of Democracy."

78. [. . .] nobody knows what they may face when the world is going through a cataclysm. I could agree with you right this minute that I don't want war, but I don't know what you might say under different conditions six months from now.

January 1940 Press Conference.

79. [. . .] the use of the word "autobiography" seems to me completely misleading. An autobiography is something that the person himself had written and taking father's own words to show a certain trend of mind is still not an autobiography because he did not write with that purpose in mind.

February 23, 1940, "My Day."

80. When life is too easy for us, we must beware or we may not be ready to meet the blows which sooner or later come to everyone, rich or poor.

February 23, 1940, "My Day."

81. You will find women divided in the same grouping that have divided men, and they approach any question before the electorate in much the same way. There are liberals and conservatives among the women as well as among the men. As far as I can judge, only one thing stands out—namely, that on the whole, during the last twenty years, government has been taking increasing cognizance of humanitarian questions, things that deal with the happiness of human beings, such as health, education, security. There is nothing, of course, to prove that this is entirely because of the women's

interests, and yet I think it is significant that this change has come about during the period when women have been exercising their franchise. It makes me surmise that women who do take an interest in public questions have thrust these interests to the fore, and obliged their fellow citizens to consider them. Whereas in the past these human problems have remained more or less in the background, today they are discussed by every governing body.

April 1940, "Women in Politics."

82. We have had, of course, a few failures among women who have taken office either because men have urged them to do so, or because they have followed in their husbands' footsteps. When a woman fails, it is much more serious than when a man fails, because the average person attributes the failure not to the individual, but to the fact that she is a woman.

April 1940, "Women in Politics."

83. It is perfectly obvious that women are not all alike. They do not think alike, nor do they feel alike on many subjects. Therefore, you can no more unite all women on a great variety of subjects than you can unite all men.

April 1940, "Women in Politics."

84. There is no reason, of course, why we should expect any woman to have the support of all women just because of her sex; but neither should women be prejudiced against women as such. We must learn to judge other women's work just as we would judge men's work, to evaluate it and to be sure that we understand and know the facts before we pass judgment.

April 1940, "Women in Politics."

85. It will always take all kinds of women to make up a world, and only now and then will they unite their interests. When they do, I think it is safe to say that something historically important will happen.

April 1940, "Women in Politics."

86. I have a great belief in spiritual force, but I think we have to realize that spiritual force alone has to have material force with it so long as we live in a material world. The two together make a strong combination.

May 17, 1940, "My Day."

87. I feel the mistakes I made serve to give me a little more wisdom and understanding in helping people who are trying today to preserve our democracy.

June 15, 1940, "Insuring Democracy."

88. [To Lorena] Mine was another day spent wondering what men do in their businesses, they are so slow on committees!

June 30, 1940, Empty Without You.

89. We will have to be very sure what we want for ourselves and our fellow citizens in order to really organize our strength and live or die for the things in which we believe.

July 3, 1940, "My Day."

90. To me there is something very contagious about the friendly atmosphere brought about by meeting old friends.

July 20, 1940, "My Day."

91. [To Lorena] I have a deep discouragement about the world these days & would like to run away from having to face it.

If I feel that way[,] what must other less [economically] secure people feel?
August 11, 1940, Empty Without You.

92. [To Lorena] I find royalty heavy & boring!
September 6, 1940, Empty Without You.

93. Hate and force cannot be in just a part of the world without having an effect on the rest of it.
September 23, 1940, "My Day."

94. [To Lorena] If F.D.R wins I'll be glad for him & for the
country & if he loses I'll be glad for myself & the kids!
October 22, 1940, Empty Without You.

95. [To Lorena] [. . .] I dread getting accustomed to 4 more
years of easy living but perhaps I can keep from being too
dependent on it. Anyway what is the use of worrying about
tomorrow let alone 4 years from now!
November 8, 1940, Empty Without You.

96. Excessive taxes produce three results as sure as sunrise.
They reduce total revenue because they invariably increase
all prices, and reduce production and employment.
November 15, 1940, "My Day."

97. I do not suppose that any really good work is ever lost.
Somewhere the seed remains and the influence is felt in the
future.
March 14, 1941, "My Day."

98. [. . .] Marriages and the upbringing of children in the
home require as well-trained a mind and as well-disciplined

a character as any other occupation that might be considered a career.

March 28, 1941, "My Day."

99. I think we ought to impress on both our girls and boys that successful marriages require just as much work, just as much intelligence and just as much unselfish devotion, as they give to any position they undertake to fill on a paid basis.

March 28, 1941, "My Day."

100. When all is said and done, it is our freedom to progress that makes us all want to live and to go on.

May 29, 1941, "My Day."

101. [To Trudy Lash] Somewhere along the line of development we discover what we really are, and then we make our real decision for which we're responsible. Make that decision primarily for yourself because you can never really live anyone else's life, not even your child's.

June 1941

102. People grow through experience if they meet life honestly and courageously. This is how character is built.

August 1, 1941, "My Day."

103. Because our nation has lived up to the rules of civilization, it will probably take us a few days to catch up with our enemy, but no one in this country will doubt the ultimate outcome.

December 8, 1941, "My Day." (The full text is in the appendix.)

104. How hard it is for human beings to learn that the only safety there is lies in being prepared for any eventuality.

December 9, 1941, "My Day."

105. [To Lorena] Our most vivid impression I think is what a blackout of an entire city really means. You get a curious feeling over here that nothing but people count.
January 5, 1942 [London], Empty Without You.

106. [telegram] MRS. FRANKLIN D. ROOSEVELT [. . .] WOULD YOU BE WILLING TO HELP OUR WAR BOND DRIVE SERVICE MOTHER'S DAY CEREMONY NEXT SATURDAY [. . .] ANNA—
May 5, 1942, Mother and Daughter.

107. [telegram] MRS. JOHN BOETTIGER [. . .] DARLING I HAVE REFUSED TO TAKE PART IN MOTHER'S DAY CELEBRATION IN NEW YORK AND NEVER WAS MUCH ON MOTHERS DAY AND COULD NOT THINK OF ANYTHING TO SAY WORTH SAYING. TERRIBLY SORRY [. . .] DEVOTEDLY [. . .] MOTHER.—
May 5, 1942, Mother and Daughter.

108. The Nazi psychology is a strange one, because fear and suffering do not create love and loyalty.
September 25, 1942, "My Day."

109. [To Lorena] The Queen showed me her own destroyed rooms here & all windows are out! It is a curious place but the people give you a sense of unity. I'm anxious to get out among them.
October 23, 1942, Empty Without You.

110. [. . .] I really believe that all men are created equal and that the "Last" Commandment, "Love thy neighbor as thyself," really means what it says.
November 26, 1942, "My Day."
Cf. Leviticus 19:18 and throughout the New Testament, such as Matthew 19:19; 22:39; 36:1.

111. We must want for others, not ourselves alone.
February 5, 1943, "My Day."

112. [To Anna] We can't take it for granted that we are the only trustworthy people in the world & we must believe in other people's intelligence & good intentions if we expect them to believe in us. That doesn't mean that we need to be weak either.
February 28, 1943, Mother and Daughter.

113. [To Anna] I don't mind spending hours on people I love but it seems such a waste when you don't care much.
March 14, 1943, Mother and Daughter.

114. One of the best ways of enslaving a people is to keep them from education and thus make it impossible for them to understand what is going on in the world as a whole. The second way of enslaving a people is to suppress the sources of information, not only by burning books but by controlling all the other ways in which ideas are transmitted.
May 11, 1943, "My Day."

115. The more we dwell on our happy memories, the better it will be for us all.
May 18, 1943, "My Day."

116. You and I may be hated by our neighbors, but if we know about it we try to change things within us which brought it about. That is the way civilized people develop [. . .]
August 13, 1943, "My Day."

117. The important thing is neither your nationality nor the religion you professed, but how your faith translated itself in your life.
September 16, 1943, "My Day."

118. I have known only a few very happy marriages. By that I do not mean just people who get along together and live contentedly through life, but people who really are excitingly happy. These people have somehow preserved the ability to rejuvenate their love so that neither the man nor the woman need wander off to find the romance they long for somewhere else.

February 8, 1944, "My Day."

119. This country of ours is unique because we have always expected every generation of young people to do better than their parents.

April 17, 1944, "My Day."

120. [. . .] every employer who forces his employees into a position where they see no way out except to strike is equally guilty with the strikers. I have seen so many condemnations of strikers, but I have seen little recognition that there are always two sides to any dispute.

June 6, 1944, "My Day."

121. Some day, perhaps, the world will be the kind of civilized place in which we can all live in safety according to our own likes. But it isn't that kind of place today, and so you and I are defended in our peaceful lives at home by those who will do what their governments ask of them, no matter what that task may be.

June 21, 1944, "My Day."

122. When the day arrives when war is no more, these men [conscientious objectors] may feel that they have hastened it. In the meantime, however, as the world is constituted today they might not be alive or they might be slaves to

other more warlike people if some of their brothers were
not willing to defend them against other warlike peoples.
June 21, 1944, "My Day."

123. [To Lorena] [. . .] [Ruth's new husband] has a cruel
face which does not seem to promise happiness for her or
for the children.
July 7, 1944, Empty Without You.

124. [To Lorena] These people [the Churchill party] are all
nice people & in some ways that is discouraging because
[if] they've not found the answers, how can we hope that
we'll find them in the future.
Quebec. September 12, 1944, Empty Without You.

125. Perhaps, in his wisdom, the Almighty is trying to show
us that a leader may chart the way, may point out the road
to lasting peace, but that many leaders and many peoples
must do the building. It cannot be the work of one man, nor
can the responsibility be laid upon his shoulders, and so,
when the time comes for people to assume the burden more
fully, he is given rest. God grant that we may have that wisdom and courage to build a peaceful world with justice and
opportunity for all people the world over.
April 17, 1945, "My Day."

126. [To Lorena] Franklin's death ended a period in history
& now in its wake those of us who laid in his shadow have
to start again under our own momentum & wonder what
we can achieve.
April 19, 1945, Empty Without You.

127. Looking at the war-torn world of today, we cannot say
that our civilization has been perfect. We can only say that

we have created greater material comfort for human beings and that we are struggling to find a way of living together peacefully and cooperatively in the future.

April 30, 1945, "My Day."

128. [. . .] in order to be useful we must stand for the things we feel are right, and we must work for those things wheresoever we find ourselves. It does very little good to believe something unless you tell your friends and associates of your beliefs.

May 7, 1945, "My Day."

129. If we give people bread, we may build friendship among the peoples of the world; and we will never have a peace without friendship around the world.

May 9, 1945, "My Day."

130. In the past we have given lip service to the desire for peace. Now we meet the test of really working to achieve something basically new in the world. Religious groups have been telling us for a long time that peace could be achieved only by a basic change in the nature of man. I am inclined to think that this is true. But if we give human beings sufficient incentive they may find good reasons for reshaping their characteristics.

August 8, 1945, "My Day."

131. This new discovery [the atomic bomb] cannot be ignored. We have only two alternative choices: destruction and death—or construction and life! If we desire our civilization to survive, then we must accept the responsibility of constructive work and of the wise use of a knowledge greater than any ever achieved by man before.

August 8, 1945, "My Day."

132. [To President Truman] "You will have pressures from every side. I am sure your own wisdom and experience and faith in God will guide you aright."
August 15, 1945, Eleanor and Harry.

133. [To Lorena] My dear, I feel more of an old lady than at 50 but I've learned to hide it better! I have more limitations but I know them & accept them! I'm going to be no leader of thought or action but a homebody in the near future & able to enjoy my friends.
September 1, 1945, Empty Without You.

134. Research and training are two things which are essential to the health of the nation. They should not depend upon private funds alone.
September 7, 1945, "My Day."

135. Being a strong nation and having the greatest physical, mental and spiritual strength today, gives us a tremendous responsibility. We cannot use our strength to coerce, but if we are big enough, I think we can lead, but it will require great vision and understanding on our part. [Letter to President Truman]
November 11, 1945, Eleanor and Harry.

136. A woman will always have to be better than a man in any job she undertakes.
November 29, 1945, "My Day."

137. [To Anna] I'm going to write the column but nothing that the press is not in on where the [UN] conference is concerned but I think there will always be personal things which can be made interesting.
December 20, 1945, Mother and Daughter.

138. All of life is a constant education.
December 22, 1945, "My Day."

139. If we hope to prosper, others prosper too, and if we hope to be trusted, we must trust others.
January 5, 1946, "My Day."

140. [Soldiers visiting Mrs. Roosevelt in London] are good boys but if they don't have enough to do they will get into trouble. That is this nature of boys, I am afraid, in any situation. [Letter to President Truman.]
January 12, 1946, Eleanor and Harry.

141. [To Anna] I think not having strong convictions they [UN legislators] doubt their ability to defend a position which they may take so they can not decide on any position and go on arguing pros and cons endlessly.
January 27, 1946, Mother and Daughter.

142. [To Anna] I'm so glad I never feel important, it does complicate life!
February 2, 1946, Mother and Daughter.

143. The whole social structure of Europe is crumbling and we might as well face the fact that leadership must come from us or it will inevitably come from Russia. [Letter to President Truman.]
March 1, 1946, Eleanor and Harry.

144. Any President frequently suffers from his friends as much as from his enemies, and it is the sense of loyalty and gratitude which often gets men in public life into the greatest of trouble. [Letter to President Truman.]
March 1, 1946, Eleanor and Harry.

145. No United Nations organization can succeed when peoples of one race approach those of other races in a spirit of contempt.

March 8, 1946, "My Day."

146. [To Anna] [One year after FDR's death] [. . .] The crowds are almost reverent as tho' they really cared deeply. . . . Very quiet, & no laughter.

April 15, 1946, Mother and Daughter.

147. [To President Truman] I cannot help feeling that we need to be firm but we haven't always been firm in the right way in our foreign policy because one can only be successfully firm, if the people one is firm with, particularly the Russians, have complete confidence in one's integrity and I am not sure that our attitude on questions like Spain and the Argentine and even in Germany itself, have been conducive to creating a feeling that we should always keep our word and that we would always talk things out absolutely sincerely before we took action.

June 1, 1946, Eleanor and Harry.

148. There is a desire for progress in the hearts of all men, and it is the sense of frustration and inability to move forward that brings violent revolution.

December 30, 1946, "My Day."

149. In a society such as ours, where changes come about easily, violent revolution is unnecessary.

December 30, 1946, "My Day."

150. Perhaps at my age [62], in any case, it is wise to curtail one's activities. One thing is sure—that if you give up any activity, it is much more difficult to start in again. [. . .]

However, at all times and as long as one lives, life adminis-
ters disciplines, and it is in accepting and obeying them that
one learns.

January 16, 1947, "My Day."

151. [To Anna] [. . .] Dr. Chiang, the delegate from China
on Human Rights [. . .] talks continually of Chinese philosophy as it influenced European 18th century thought & I
see blank looks around the table among the South American & Russian group who don't care much about ancient
philosophy! . . .

February 19, 1947, Mother and Daughter.

152. [To President Truman] [. . .] in a press conference I
said that I felt ways had to be found to get on with Russia.
That does not mean we have to appease Russia. I do not
believe the Russians want to go to war. Neither do we but
I think the ingenuity to find ways to get what we want
rests with us.

June 7, 1947, Eleanor and Harry.

153. [To President Truman] There is too much to be done in
the world to allow for resentments.

June 7, 1947, Eleanor and Harry.

154. [To Anna] One is so far away here that wars & rumors
of wars seem to recede into the background & yet I am really discouraged over Russia's attitude on the Marshall
Plan & find it hard to understand. Elliott feels they think we
won't come through but even that makes no sense to me for
they are furnishing their reasons why we shouldn't!

July 19, 1947, Mother and Daughter.

155. [. . .] if, in the course of the years, I have gained any wisdom whatsoever, it is the wisdom to know that the Kingdom of God must come on earth through the efforts of human beings and that war in the atomic age will simply mean annihilation, certainly not evolution. With age has come also a capacity for patience; rooted beliefs in certain fundamental things, but an ability to try to understand the motivations of other people; and a kind of interest in human beings which allows for no bitterness towards any person.

July 24, 1947, "My Day."

156. Peace has to begin within each individual's heart and has to be lived by each of us every day.

August 30, 1947, "My Day."

157. [To Anna] John [Boettiger] told me how you feel about my remarks on [Henry A.] Wallace and the 1940 Convention. I think I did not explain sufficiently carefully and I will talk it over when I see you which I hope will be soon. I want any other criticisms that you have, as so often it is a case of knowing things and not expressing them well. It is very valuable to me to get the impact of what is written on someone else.

October 10, 1947 to Bernard M. Baruch, Mother and Daughter.

158. The people take longer to enjoy life as they live it here [Paris], and I am not sure they may not get more of it than we do at home.

1948, "My Day."

159. To live deeply requires a capacity for feeling—and that, too, is something which must be developed. For the most part people's emotions, when untrained and uncontrolled,

are apt only to stir the surface and not to reflect themselves in thought and action.

January 7, 1948, "My Day."

160. I can quite understand why men like Prof. [Albert] Einstein feel that a world government would answer the problem, but any of us who have worked in the United Nations realize that we will have to learn to crawl before we learn to walk. If the great nations find it so hard to agree on the minor points at issue today, how do any of these hopeful people think that a world government could be made to work? People have to want to get on together and to do away with force, but so far there are many throughout the world who have not advanced to the point of really wanting to do this.

January 29, 1948, "My Day."

161. [To President Truman] No one won the last war, and no one will win the next war.

March 22, 1948, Eleanor and Harry.

162. [To David] [. . .] The people I love mean more to me than all the public things even if you do think that public affairs should be my vocation. I only do the public things because I really love all people and I only love all people because there are few close people whom I love dearly and who matter to me above everything else.

April 17, 1948, Kindred Souls.

163. [To Anna] Last night [. . .] the Welfare Minister sitting by me said "We do not think of the war. There is work to do day by day & we do it." Not such a bad motto for life is it?

April 20, 1948, Mother and Daughter.

164. [To Anna] What friends Father [FDR] made every-where for the U.S. It ought to bring tangible results to us in the future if we are wise.

April 20, 1948 [in Holland] Mother and Daughter.

165. [To David, referring to the illness from which he was recovering, she wrote] Of course you have grown under this experience and everything met and accepted and con-quered gives you greater confidence.

May 26, 1948, Kindred Souls.

166. [To Anna] Perhaps when things [...] happen which seem just too much to bear, we are being given a lesson in values. There is no use trying to teach the weak but the strong are worth training. When a child is ill you know that the other losses were of little importance, his life & happi-ness is all that counts. You work to repay money losses to others because you have a sense of integrity & responsibil-ity. You work for some future security so as not to be a bur-den on the young but you learn that the satisfaction that comes are in doing the work well & in making those you love happy.

August 28, 1948, Mother and Daughter.

167. There is a certain kind of healthy vulgarity that one can endure, perhaps with some embarrassment but still with amusement. There are certain other types of artistic and emotional expression, however, that show degeneracy of the spirit with the individual and with the nation.

September 21, 1948, "My Day."

168. One amendment [to the proposed Universal Declara-tion of Human Rights] [...] created a great effect upon a

number of the members of the committee. I immediately asked to speak, but now I think it was fortunate—[. . .] that the opportunity was not given to me yesterday. I now realize I would have spoken with too much emotion and perhaps not as objectively as the conditions called for.

October 9, 1948, "My Day."

169. I would have been delighted to see in the preamble [to the Universal Declaration of Human Rights] a paragraph alluding to the Supreme Power. I knew very well, however, there were many men around the table [at the UN] who would violently be opposed to naming God, and I did not want to put it to a [roll call] because I thought for those of us who are Christians it would be rather difficult to have God defeated in a vote.

December 10, 1948, "My Day."

170. [To President Truman] We are engaged in the war for peace in which there enter questions of world economy, food, religion, education, health, and social conditions, as well as military and power conditions.

December 28, 1948, Eleanor and Harry.

171. [To David] [. . .] as one gets older the joy of real companionableness is rarer and rarer especially with the young and one cares for fewer and fewer people.

1949, Kindred Souls.

172. [To David] [. . .] I have lived many emotions and observed many and I am sure happy marriages develop when the man shows his desire to the woman and she responds fully and happily.

1949, Kindred Souls.

173. It is curious to realize that out of my years in Washington, though I met many people and learned much about the country and its people, I made very few new friends. [...] I have kept pleasant memories but I have deep-rooted ties with none. [...] On the whole, however, I think I lived those years very impersonally. It was almost as though I had erected someone a little outside of myself who was the president's wife. I was lost somewhere deep down inside myself.

1949, This I Remember.

174. Although no human being ever completely knows another human being, one cannot live for many years with a person without learning something about him.

1949, This I Remember.

175. [...] I seldom told them (my sons) what was right or what was wrong. The reason I didn't was that I was never sure I knew myself.

1949, This I Remember.

176. I do not question that I often gave [money] to people who were not worthy; but in those years it seemed better to take that risk than to fail those who were worthy.

1949, This I Remember.

177. Nothing we learn in this world is ever wasted and I have come to the conclusion that practically nothing we do ever stands by itself. If it is good, it will serve some good purpose in the future. If it is evil, it may haunt us and handicap our efforts in unimagined ways.

1949, This I Remember.

178. I always worried about whether anyone was being ne-glected and whether there was enough food, or whether something else might be wrong. I never was able to forget about things, to take them naturally and enjoy myself, and to let other people worry. It would I am sure have been just as effective.

1949, This I Remember.

179. It is a pity that we can not have the experience that comes with age in our younger days, when we really need it. We certainly would enjoy life more and I am sure that somehow the responsibilities would all be taken care of quite as well.

1949, This I Remember.

180. My only interest in jewelry is a sentimental interest in having something that has belonged in the family or that has been worn by someone I really care about or that is given to me by someone I love. I like beautiful things, but it would never occur to me to go out and spend money on jewelry to wear when there is already so much in the family.

1949, This I Remember.

181. I can be calm and quiet [in a crisis], but it takes all the discipline I have acquired in life to keep on talking and smiling and to concentrate on the conversation addressed to me. I want to be left alone while I store up fortitude for what I fear may be a blow of fate. However, I have learned to feel one way inside at such times and outwardly to go on like an automaton.

1949, This I Remember.

182. I have never known what it was to be bored or to have time hang heavily on my hands. It has always been difficult

to find time to do the things I want to do. When I was young I read a great deal, but during these last years I have had to read so many things that those I should like to read are too often neglected. Sometimes I think it would be delightful if an afternoon or evening could actually be given to uninterrupted reading for pure pleasure.

1949, This I Remember.

183. When I do not know the answer to a question and cannot find it, I say so frankly.

1949, This I Remember.

184. It is useless to resent anything in this world; one must learn to look on whatever happens as part of one's education in life and make it serve a good purpose in the formation of character.

1949, This I Remember.

185. I had already learned never to ask questions when information was not volunteered, and it became almost an obsession with me as the war went on. I was conscious of the fact that because I saw a great many people I might let slip something that should not be told, so I used to beg my husband to tell me no secrets. Many times it was impossible not to know something was afoot, but if I made no effort to find out what, my knowledge was pretty vague.

1949, This I Remember.

186. To appear to be on the inside and know more than others about what is going on is a great temptation for most people. It is a rare person who is willing to seem to know less than he does or who is honest enough to say: "I saw the president and he told me nothing that had the slightest sig-

nificance." Somehow, people seem to feel that it is belittling to their importance not to know more than other people.

1949, This I Remember.

187. Sorrow in itself and the loss of someone whom you love is hard to bear, but when sorrow is mixed with regret and a consciousness of waste there is added a touch of bitterness which is even more difficult to carry day in and day out.

1949, This I Remember.

188. It is curious how at such times [as on Pearl Harbor day] one's anxiety for the nation and one's personal anxiety merge as one goes over and over all the things that have happened and may happen. For a woman, the personal side comes more strongly to the fore.

1949, This I Remember.

189. At the end of the twelve years [in the White House] I was still doing what I thought were casual things without ever realizing how momentous apparently they seemed to other people.

1949, This I Remember.

190. To explain to one's country that there must be a long period while the military forces are being trained and armed, during which production will be one of the most important factors, and that meanwhile people must be patient and hope at best "to hold the line," is no easy or popular thing to do. I always had great admiration for the way in which Mr. Churchill did this. In some ways he was more blunt with the people of Great Britain than my husband ever was with us. The British people were closer to the danger and I suppose for that very reason could better understand the blunt approach.

1949, This I Remember.

191. I suppose the saving fact for all human beings [. . .] is that they never think anything is going happen to them until it actually happens. Theoretically and intellectually they recognize the possibility, but in my own case, at least, it was not a sign of courage that I went ahead and did certain things which might have had some slight danger attached to them. It was simply that, like most human beings, I am not given to seeing myself disappear off the face of the earth. If it should happen, having no choice, I would, I hope, accept the inevitable philosophically.

1949, This I Remember.

192. Though certain situations might be unfamiliar and give me a feeling of inadequacy and of not knowing the proper way to behave, still I would do my best and not worry.

1949, This I Remember.

193. I imagine every mother felt as I did when I said good-bye to the children during the war. I had a feeling that I might be saying good-bye for the last time. It was a sort of precursor of what it would be like if your children were killed and never to come back. Life had to go on and you had to do what was required of you, but something inside of you quietly died. I began to look with wonder at all the women in the country who must be feeling this same way and I came to admire their courage. Fathers had the same kind of courage, but there was a greater acceptance on their part of the need for war and perhaps a greater pride in the fact that their sons were fulfilling their duty. Men do not instinctively revolt against war as women do.

1949, This I Remember.

194. Many of the [. . .] boys I saw in hospitals are now leading happy and useful lives, but they carry with them, day after day, the results of the war. The gallantry of youth,

bearing handicaps which will be a cross all their lives, seems to me a theme for some great poet. Though the war had to be fought to preserve our freedom, their full reward for their suffering is not yet in sight. To see that it is paid in full measure is an obligation which all of us who lived through the war owe to the thousands who fought it. If we do not achieve the real ends for which they sacrificed—a peaceful world in which there exists freedom from fear both of aggression and want—we have failed. This is the challenge presented to the citizens of our democracy by the last war and we shall not have paid our debt until these ends are achieved.

1949, This I Remember.

195. Shortly after my birthday I went at the regular interval to donate blood to the Red Cross. The young lady at the desk was terribly embarrassed because I had passed the sixty mark in years and no one over sixty could be allowed to give blood. I was slightly indignant, because I was unable to see how in a few weeks my blood could have changed; I realized, however that there had to be some definite limit set, and so I felt I really entered old age on October 11, 1944.

1949, This I Remember.

196. All human beings have failings, all human beings have needs and temptations and stresses. Men and women who live together through long years get to know one another's failings; but they also come to know what is worthy of respect and admiration in those they live with and in themselves. If at the end one can say: "This man used to the limit the powers that God granted him; he was worthy of love and respect and of the sacrifices of many people, made in order that he might achieve what he deemed to be

his task," then that life has been lived well and there are no regrets.

1949, This I Remember.

197. I sometimes wonder whether I really wanted Franklin to run [in 1928]. I imagine I accepted his nomination and later his election as I had accepted most of the things that had happened in life thus far: one did whatever seemed necessary and adjusted one's personal life to the developments in other people's lives.

1949, This I Remember.

198. There are two kinds of snobbishness. That of the man who has had a good many opportunities and looks down on those who lack them is usually recognized by all. The other kind of snobbishness is rarely understood, yet it is real. It is that of the self-made man, who glories in his success in overcoming difficulties and admires greatly people who have achieved the things he considers of importance.

1949, This I Remember.

199. At one point, I received a wire from Franklin: "Hope you have a good trip. What shall I do with your casket?" I puzzled over this for some time and it finally dawned on me that I had forgotten one piece of my luggage—a lunch basket! It was, of course, a typographical error, but that message remained a family joke for many years, and we told my husband he was preparing for any contingency.

1949, This I Remember.

200. The loss of a generation [in war] makes itself felt acutely twenty to twenty-five years later, when many men who would have been leaders are just not there to lead.

1949, This I Remember.

201. A man who chooses to hold public office must learn to accept the slander as part of the job and to trust that the majority of the people will judge him by his accomplishments in public service.

1949, This I Remember.

202. Always in Franklin there was evident a sense of humor, which could turn the most serious subject into an object of fun at times when he thought those around him needed a little break in the tension or perhaps a reminder that they were not so important as they thought; for one can reach a point where one's importance looms so great that one simply cannot carry the responsibility. This was at the bottom of many jokes that he sometimes aimed at himself, as well as at others.

1949, This I Remember.

203. I have never known a man who gave one a greater sense of security [than Franklin]. That was because I never heard him say there was a problem that he thought it was impossible for human beings to solve. He recognized the difficulties and often said that while he did not know the answer, he was completely confident that there was an answer; that somewhere a man could be found who could give the answer, and that one had to try until one either found it for oneself or got it through someone else. He never talked about his doubts. When he was planning something he consulted many people and took the best advice he could get, but once he had made his decision he wasted no time in worry.

1949, This I Remember.

204. I believe it was from his faith in the people that he [Franklin] drew the words of his first inaugural address: "The only thing we have to fear, is fear itself."

1949, This I Remember.

205. The essentials in an important speech must remain, because it is necessary to get in everything that will clarify the subject; yet it must not be complicated by the addition of even one unnecessary word.

1949, This I Remember.

206. If I liked his [Franklin's] speech after he delivered it, I always said so; if for any reason I disapproved of it, I said nothing. But I never expected him to pay any attention to my ideas—he was much too good a speaker to need any advice from me.

1949, This I Remember.

207. Though Franklin always said I was far too impatient ever to be a good politician, and though my sense of timing is nowhere near so trustworthy as his was, I have grown more patient with age and have perhaps learned from my husband that no leader can be too far ahead of his followers. Also I think my observations of conditions and of the feelings of the average people within our country are fairly trustworthy.

1949, This I Remember.

208. [. . .] I tried to concentrate on faces and to recognize as many as I could, because being a little deaf I never really heard names. [. . .] However, when there are a great many people, toward the end faces become blurred. Once I walked into the dining room after the receiving was over and saw two old friends. "Where did you come from?" I said, and they told me they had gone through the line and that I had shaken hands with them warmly.

1949, This I Remember.

209. The kudos that goes with public office is essential to obtain good men. In a way it is a recognition of the sacri-

fices that men or women who enter public service must make. In addition, it maintains respect for the office itself.
1949, This I Remember.

210. The question has never been decided whether a human being acquires more characteristics through heredity or through environment. Nevertheless I am quite sure that human beings who live in the Washington slums are conditioned to a great extent by their environment.
April 22, 1949, "My Day."

211. [. . .] I would not choose [*Death of a Salesman*] as entertainment or for its moral lesson. That lesson, in more realistic style, you can find in many an American community. I think I like it better when it points to the fact that a man, if finally brought to face the truth, can pick himself up and create a different ending.
April 28, 1949, "My Day."

212. We are proud people, conscious of our greatness, and yet our traditions of simplicity are important to us. We want dignity but no false pomp and show.
May 18, 1949, "My Day."

213. [I think] religious education was valuable to every child, but it could not be given in the school alone. The home and the church must cooperate.
July 13, 1949, "My Day."

214. There is no real reason why every school should not teach every child that one of the important aspects of our life is its spiritual side. It might be possible to devise a prayer that all the denominations could say and it certainly ought to be possible to read certain verses from the Bible every day. It probably would do children no harm to learn

to know some of the writings of the great religious leaders who have led other great religious movements.

July 15, 1949, "My Day."

215. I think if we care for the preservation of our liberties we must allow all people, whether we disagree with them or not, to hold meetings and express their views unmolested as long as they do not advocate the overthrow of our government by force.

September 3, 1949, "My Day."

216. One must look on a portrait as something to make future generations feel that they do not have to be too much ashamed of their forebears.

December 16, 1949, "My Day."

1950–1959

Time Line

1950 Second volume of FDR letters is published. See 1948.

1951 Mrs. Roosevelt writes the introduction to the autobiography of Helen Keller.

1952 Adlai Stevenson runs against Dwight D. Eisenhower for president and is strongly supported by Mrs. Roosevelt. After the election of Eisenhower, she resigns from the United Nations delegation. She writes the foreword to *A Fair World for All* by Dorothy Fisher, on the meaning of the Declaration of Human Rights.

1953 As equality for women in the Democratic National Convention is advanced, and as the Women's Division in which Mrs. Roosevelt served for over thirty years is no longer needed, it is abolished.

1954 Mrs. Roosevelt writes the introduction to Lela Stiles's *The Man Behind Roosevelt*, a study of Louis McHenry Howe.

1956 Mrs. Roosevelt becomes very actively involved in Adlai Stevenson's second unsuccessful bid for the presidency.

1957 Mrs. Eleanor Roosevelt interviews Nikita Khrushchev in the Soviet Union for the *New York Post*. "F.D.R. as seen by Eleanor Roosevelt," appears in the journal *Wisdom*.

1959 Mrs. Eleanor Roosevelt hosts a visit of Khrushchev to Hyde Park.

Quotations

217. [Mrs. Roosevelt recommended to President Truman that the poem "The Calf Path" by Sam Walter Foss (1858–1911) from *The Home Book of Verse* be read to all senators.]

For men are prone to go it blind
Along the calf-paths of the mind,
And work away from sun to sun
To do what other men have done . . .
But how wise old wood-gods laugh,
Who saw the first primeval calf . . .
For thus such reverence is lent
To well-established precedent.
                    March 21, 1950, Eleanor and Harry.

218. [. . .] the collective intelligence of mankind should be able to save the world from suicide, and yet nothing seems to indicate that such is the case. We follow the paths of the years gone by and we feel a little of the inevitableness of the Greek tragedy.
                    December 20, 1950, "My Day."

219. [To David] Marriages are two-way streets and when they are not happy both must be willing to adjust. Both must love.
                    1951, Kindred Souls.

220. We cannot afford to waste brains in this country. They are becoming more important to us everyday. And surely

financial position should not bar young people from the education which can give them positions of leadership in our nation in the future.

February 22, 1951, "My Day."

221. [To President Truman] I think the great nations, but especially the United States, have got to understand that there is a feeling in the world of a desire to attain some kind of a better standard of living and they feel that particularly the United States has an obligation to make the plans and help them to carry them out to apply those standards.

May 27, 1951, Eleanor and Harry.

222. [To President Truman] The reason they go all out on economic and social rights in the Human Rights Commission is because those are the rights that mean something tangible to them in their every day lives. They do not expect them to be achieved overnight, but they use the word "right" in a different sense than we do legally.

May 27, 1951, Eleanor and Harry.

223. Almost always the male animal is the show-off while the female remains demure and is less startlingly clad. Perhaps someday we will have the courage to strike a good medium and let the men have a little self-expression in their clothes.

July 13, 1951, "My Day."

224. One must even beware of too much certainty that the answers to life's problems can only be found in one way and that all must agree to search for light in the same way and cannot find it in any other way.

November 22, 1951, "My Day."

225. [Address to the 1952 UN convention] To achieve peace we must recognize the historic truth that we can no longer live apart from the rest of the world. We must also recognize the fact that peace, like freedom, is not won once and for all. It is fought for daily, in many small acts, and is the result of many individual efforts. [. . .] We should remember that the United Nations is not a cure-all. It is only an instrument capable of effective action when its members have a will to make it work.

1952, quoted in Eleanor and Harry.

226. [To President Truman] The recognition of any church as a temporal power puts that church in a different position from any of the other churches and while we are now only hearing from the Protestant groups, the Moslems may one day wake up to this and make an equal howl. For us who take a firm stand on the separation of church and state, the recognition of a temporal power seems inconsistent.

January 29, 1952, Eleanor and Harry.

227. [Letter to President Truman from India] The problem here (in India) is much the same as that of China, though in Nehru we have a leader of infinitely higher quality than Chiang. Mr. Nehru has around him a great many good men. Gandhi has left his mark and there is an unselfish service being given among young and old which might be of help even in our own democracy.

March 7, 1952, Eleanor and Harry.

228. [Letter to President Truman] Most of us would like to see exclusionist bars go down but not in favor of new ones which would provide fresh evidence that we consider ourselves "superior" to the peoples of Asia.

May 31, 1952, Eleanor and Harry.

229. [. . .] no one likes the rich uncle who flaunts his wealth in the face of your poverty; who will help you, perhaps—but on his own terms; who will send you to college, if you like—but only to the college of his choice. This, of course, is not a fair description of our attitude; but, nevertheless, fair or not, it is the way many people see us.

1953, India and the Awakening East.

230. The new Constitution [in India] abolishes Untouchability and guarantees all people equal rights before the law. But, as we know in our own country, it is one thing to abolish discrimination in the Constitution and another to put it into nation-wide practice [. . .].

1953, India and the Awakening East.

231. It was at the Sherif's receptions [in Bombay] that, when I found I could not possibly shake hands with everyone present, I used for the first time the Indians greeting, putting my hands together in front of me and bowing, as I had seen the Indian women do. [. . .] I was asked to go out on the balcony and greet the huge crowd that had gathered outside the hotel. Again there was nothing I could do except repeat the gesture as I looked down at the people, but it seemed to please them very much.

1953, India and the Awakening East.

232. Obviously, in any country where the point of view of self-interest prevails, the enlightened leaders are going to have an uphill job in instituting permanent and far-reaching reforms.

1953, India and the Awakening East.

233. As long as I live I shall carry in my mind the beauty of the Taj, and at last I know why my father felt it was the one

unforgettable thing he had seen in India. He always said it was the one thing he wanted us to see together.

1953, India and the Awakening East.

234. One does not want to talk and one cannot glibly say this is a beautiful thing, but one's silence, I think, says this is a beauty that enters the soul.

1953, India and the Awakening East.

235. I do not know whether my analysis is right or whether I am simply imagining a situation; yet when I was talking to [Prime Minister] Nehru that night, he gave me no feeling that I was wrong.

1953, India and the Awakening East.

236. [. . .] the Horatio Alger story and all its implications about the American way would, I am afraid, be totally unintelligible to most of the people of India.

1953, India and the Awakening East.

237. An understanding of our own spiritual foundations may be one of the bridges we need to better understanding of the East and its people.

1953, India and the Awakening East.

238. One word I think I must say about the role that needs to be played by the citizens of the United States. Somehow we must be able to show people that democracy is not words, but action.

1953, India and the Awakening East.

239. We must, of course, tell the truth and acknowledge our failures, but we should constantly cite examples showing that we are continually planning and striving for a more perfect democracy.

1953, India and the Awakening East.

240. We must show by our behavior that we believe in equality and justice and that our religion teaches faith and love and charity to our fellow men. Here is where each of us has a job to do that must be done at home, because we can lose the battle on the soil of the United States just as surely as we can lose it in any one of the other countries of the world. [. . .]

1953, India and the Awakening East.

241. [. . .] I shall never cease to hope that I may awaken in others a sense of the importance of these nations to the future of the world and a realization that we have strong potential friends there. We shall have to be willing to learn and to accept differences of opinion and background, for they will not always think and feel as we do, nor will they always accept our solutions to their problems. But if we try to understand them, they will, I think, come to understand us and to believe in us, and in our genuine desire to help them. For in the end we all want the same thing. We all want peace.

1953, India and the Awakening East.

242. In the United Nations we are making an effort to work out the technique of living in harmony; and I have come to feel with ever-increasing conviction that work with and through the United Nations is the keystone to success in developing co-operation among countries and to peace in the future.

1953, India and the Awakening East.

243. [. . .] the Moslems of Lebanon are [. . .] as deeply conscious of the Islamic tie as the Moslems anywhere else. There, as in other Arab lands, one is aware always of religion of Mohammed as a pervasive, sometimes subtle, but powerful force. This may not be an altogether happy situa-

tion for us, any more than it is, in my opinion, for them. Nevertheless, we had better be aware of it and watch it. For just as the Soviet Union has made a religion out of a political creed—communism—so, by a kind of reverse twist, the followers of Islam have made their religion an integral and controlling part of their political life.

1953, India and the Awakening East.

244. All one can do is to get the Arab point of view in the Arab countries, the Israeli point of view in Israel, balance them against each other and against one's own background of information.

1953, India and the Awakening East.

245. Though I appreciated the official solicitude for my well-being, I could not bring myself to believe that all these precautions were really necessary and when I finally insisted on dispensing with my armed guard I am afraid they credited me with being either unwarrantably courageous or foolhardy.

1953, India and the Awakening East.

246. Prejudices and feelings must be put aside and the whole refugee problem looked upon as an economic one.

1953, India and the Awakening East.

247. [. . .] though Moslem law permits a man to have four wives, it stipulates that he may not favor one at the expense of the others. (I gather from the Moslem ladies to whom I talked that a trend toward monogamy was definitely indicated, since, under present conditions it was going to be increasingly difficult to persuade four women that they were all being treated equally well.)

1953, India and the Awakening East.

248. What Gandhi said about India is something for every one of us to ponder. Most of us are constantly concerned about material things and yet the people whom we like best to have with us and who make the best impression on those with whom they come in contact are the people who rarely give much thought to material things. Their minds dwell on the deeper questions of life.
January 27, 1953, "My Day."

249. [. . .] The more we simplify our material needs the more we are free to think of other things.
January 27, 1953, "My Day."

250. You rarely attain finality. If you did life would be over, but as you strive new visions open before you, new possibilities for the satisfaction of living.
March 3, 1953, "My Day."

251. One does not weep for those who die, particularly when they have lived a full life. And I doubt in any case whether the gauge of love and sorrow is in the tears that are shed in the first days of mourning. People who remain with you in your daily life, even though they are no longer physically present, who are frequently in your mind, often mentioned, part of your laughter, part of your joy—they are the people you really miss. They are the people from whom you are never quite separated. You do not need to walk heavily all your life to really miss people.
April 14, 1953, "My Day."

252. I have seen women become a great influence in their neighborhood, both in city and rural areas, just because they had free time to undertake a number of little civic, church or philanthropic chores—things that none of the younger women felt they had the time to accomplish.
1954, "My Day."

253. It seems to me that the discovery of this latest bomb has actually outlawed the use of atomic bombs. The power of destruction is so great that unless we face the fact that no one in the world can possibly use it and therefore it must be outlawed as a weapon, we risk putting an end to civilization.

April 16, 1954, "My Day."

254. One can no longer lay down rules as to what individuals will do in any area of their lives in a world that is changing as fast as ours is changing today.

May 20, 1954, "My Day."

255. One of the essential steps that must be taken throughout the world is for individuals to try to set their own houses in order, to get rid of feelings of hate and to try to develop charity and understanding in the circles that they individually touch.

August 25, 1954, "My Day."

256. It seems to me that men who have had a purpose, and have really worked for it, come to their older years still with a vitality and an interest in life which is lacking in those who have been less dedicated.

November 21, 1954, "My Day."

257. The woman who dresses to suit her particular type, with only a moderate bowing acquaintance with fashion, comes out better than the woman who is a slave to the designer of the moment.

December 3, 1954, "My Day."

258. I consider those are rich who are doing something they feel worthwhile and which they enjoy doing.

March 9, 1955, "My Day."

259. [To President Truman] While here [Tel Aviv, Israel] I have been constantly reminded of the fact that my husband told me at one time that these Eastern countries had so many problems he would like to come here after he retired and try to help solve them. I protested at the time that we had enough problems of our own but I felt I should find myself traveling to this part of the world and spending a good deal of time here.

March 26, 1955, Eleanor and Harry.

260. Our doctors had better start finding out why men wear out faster than women and they had better keep them alive for the happiness and contentment of all.

May 13, 1955, "My Day."

261. [To Lorena] Of course you will forget the sad times at the end & eventually think only of the pleasant memories. Life is like that, with ends that have to be forgotten.

August 9, 1955, Empty Without You.

262. More people are affected by the occupation of a house-wife and mother than are ever touched by any single business, no matter how large it may be.

October 17, 1955, "My Day."

263. If women really understand the issues they will probably talk more effectively to their neighbors than any of the men, especially if the issues are such that they affect their daily lives.

December 7, 1955, "My Day."

264. [To David] Love must be given freely and not look for any return, it is only pride that makes one crave a return.

1956, Kindred Souls.

265. Intermarriage of races does not of necessity follow the granting of equal opportunity, for marriage is a purely personal matter.

May 5, 1956, "My Day."

266. Leaflets were dropped over Hiroshima before the attack, warning the people to leave the city, and the same thing was done at Nagasaki. But it is human nature to stay where you are and not believe the worst until it happens.

May 31, 1956, "My Day."

267. [Address to the Democratic National Convention] It is true we have differences, but everywhere in our country we know that today our differences must somehow be resolved, because we stand before the world on trial, really, to show what democracy means, and that is a heavy responsibility, because the world today is deciding between democracy and Communism, and one means freedom and one means slavery.

August 13, 1956, Eleanor and Harry.

268. [Address to the Democratic National Convention] Great leaders we have had, but we could not have had great leaders unless they had a great people to follow. You cannot be a great leader unless the people are great. That is what I want to remind every one of you tonight. You must be a great people with great objectives.

August 13, 1956, Eleanor and Harry.

269. [Address to the Democratic National Convention] I remember very well the first crisis that we met in '32, and I remember that we won out, because the people were ready to carry their share of the burden, and follow and carry through the words, *"All you have to fear, the only thing you have to fear, is fear itself."*

August 13, 1956, Eleanor and Harry.

270. We do not like to be told that we have ghettos in our big cities, but that is exactly what we have, and we will continue to have them until we get over the idea that we cannot live in the same houses and share all public facilities on an equal basis with all of our citizens.

January 26, 1957, "My Day."

271. We must join in an effort to use all knowledge for the good of all human beings. When we do that we shall have nothing to fear.

1958, On My Own.

272. It's good to be middle-aged. Things don't matter so much. You don't take it so hard when things happen to you that you don't like. [. . .] I have never been bored, never found the days long enough for the range of activities with which I wanted to fill them. And having learned to stare down fear, I long ago reached the point where there is no living person whom I fear, and few challenges that I am not willing to face.

1958, The Autobiography of Eleanor Roosevelt.

273. I say to the young: "Do not stop thinking of life as an adventure. You have no security unless you can live bravely, excitingly, imaginatively."

1958, The Autobiography of Eleanor Roosevelt.

274. Life was meant to be lived, and curiosity must be kept alive. One must never, for whatever reason, turn his back on life.

1958, The Autobiography of Eleanor Roosevelt.

275. [October 5, 1957 to Khrushchev] Not the people, but the governments, make war. And then they persuade the people that it is in a good cause, the cause of their own defense.

March 27, 1958, "My Day."

276. You like to respect and admire someone whom you love, but actually you often love even more the people who require understanding and who make mistakes and have to grow with their mistakes.

March 27, 1958, "My Day."

277. I can remember my mother-in-law saying, "Why don't you tell the children that is wrong?" And I weakly responded, "Because I am not quite sure that in certain circumstances it is wrong."

March 27, 1958, "My Day."

278. Arts in every field—music, drama, sculpture, painting—we can learn to appreciate and enjoy. We need not be artists, but we should be able to appreciate the work of artists. But these things must be taught, and in the age now developing about us.

November 5, 1958, "My Day."

279. [Talk at a Democratic fund-raiser dinner in honor of her 75th birthday, introduced by Truman, at the Waldorf-Astoria Hotel] We will make mistakes. But if we make them and are willing to acknowledge them and to change, that will mean that we will, in the end, succeed.

1959, Eleanor and Harry.

280. Strength that goes wrong is even more dangerous than weakness that goes wrong.

April 28, 1959, "My Day."

281. The separation of church and state is extremely important to any of us who hold to the original traditions of our nation. To change these traditions by changing our tradi-

tional attitude toward public education would be harmful, I think to our whole attitude of tolerance in the religious area.
June 23, 1959, "My Day." See also Eleanor and Harry.

282. [To President Truman] I would give a great deal, [. . .] if we could come to an agreement for stopping the whole use of atomic energy for military purposes.
August 12, 1959, Eleanor and Harry.

1960–1962

Time Line

1960 Mrs. Roosevelt begins to be actively involved in the presidential campaign of John F. Kennedy after his visit with her at Val-Kill. She writes the introduction to her autobiography. She adds material to *The Search for Understanding*.

1961 *The Autobiography of Eleanor Roosevelt* is published. It brings together *This Is My Story* (1937), *This I Remember* (1949), *On My Own* (1958), and *The Search for Understanding* (1958).

1961 Mrs. Roosevelt is appointed by President Kennedy to the United Nations. He also names her the first chairperson of the President's Commission on the Status of Women.

1962 Mrs. Roosevelt chairs the influential ad hoc commission of inquiry into the administration of justice in civil rights.

Mrs. Roosevelt dies on November 7, 1962, in New York City, of complications stemming from tuberculosis reactivated by pharmaceuticals prescribed to treat anemia.

Quotations

283. Mr. Nixon never has anything but hindsight.
1960, "My Day."

284. Religious freedom cannot just mean Protestant freedom; it must be freedom for all religions.
1960, "My Day."

285. Do the things that interest you and do them with all your heart. Don't be concerned about whether people are watching you or criticizing you. The chances are that they aren't paying attention to you.
1960, You Learn by Living.

286. For almost every achievement in life, it is essential to deal with other people. [. . .] It is only by inducing others to go along that changes are accomplished and work is done.
1960, You Learn by Living.

287. Your ambition should be to get as much life out of living as you possibly can, as much enjoyment, as much interest, as much experience, as much understanding. Not simply to be what is generally called a "success."
1960, You Learn by Living.

288. I am convinced that every effort must be made in childhood to teach the young to use their own minds. For one thing is sure: If they don't make up their minds, someone will do it for them.
1960, You Learn by Living.

289. I think it is essential that you should teach your child that he has an intellectual and spiritual obligation to decide

for himself what he thinks and not to allow himself to accept what comes from others without putting it through his own reasoning process.

1960, You Learn by Living.

290. It is never enough, it seems to me, to teach a child mere information. In the first place, we have to face the fact that no one can acquire all there is to learn about any subject. What is essential is to train the mind so that it is capable of finding facts as it needs them, train it to learn how to learn.

1960, You Learn by Living.

291. One of the problems all parents face is that of bringing up their children to be as free of fear as possible. Certainly you can't accomplish this unless you have developed a philosophy for yourself that is freed from fear. If you can give them a trust in God, they will have one sure way of meeting all the uncertainties of existence.

1960, You Learn by Living.

292. The children will accept the standards their parents have set as examples. But, if it is all talk, if the parents say one thing and do another, the children will be antagonistic and will care nothing about what their parents want them to do.

1960, You Learn by Living.

293. We all create the person we become by our choices as we go through life. In a very real sense, by the time we are adults, we are the sum total of the choices we have made.

1960, You Learn by Living.

294. The chief duty of the citizen is to make his government the best possible medium for the peaceful and prosperous conduct of life.

1960, You Learn by Living.

295. Often a man will have to face a choice: Will you stand firmly for a certain principle and risk defeat, or will you compromise on the issue so you will not be defeated and will still have an opportunity to accomplish other things?

1960, You Learn by Living.

296. No man is defeated without until he has first been defeated within.

1960, You Learn by Living.

297. In today's life you must have convictions. You must make up your mind on where you stand. In the company of your own peers you should be prepared to state where you stand and defend your opinion. It is not enough to say, "I do not agree at all." You must be able to say why.

1960, You Learn by Living.

298. Courage is more exhilarating than fear and in the long run it is easier. We do not have to become heroes overnight. Just a step at a time, meeting each thing that comes up, seeing it is not as dreadful as it appeared, discovering we have the strength to stare it down.

1960, You Learn by Living.

299. It is not our job to change people's customs. It is our job to know what they are and, if possible, to understand them.

1960, You Learn by Living.

300. I happen to think that a belief in God is all that is necessary for the acceptance of death, since you know that death, like life, is part of God's pattern.

1960, You Learn by Living.

301. Often people have asked me, "How do you recover from disaster?" I don't know any answer but the obvious one. You do it by meeting it and going on. From each you learn something, from each you acquire additional strength and confidence in yourself to meet the next one when it comes.

1960, You Learn by Living.

302. Unless indoctrinated, a child is too logical to understand discrimination. It is the duty of every self-respecting citizen to oppose the prejudiced indoctrination of children.

1960, You Learn by Living.

303. What I have learned from my own experience is that the most important ingredients in a child's education are curiosity, interest, imagination, and a sense of the adventure of life.

1960, You Learn by Living.

304. As I look back, I think probably the factor which influenced me most in my early years was an avid desire, even before I was aware what I was doing, to experience all I could as deeply as I could.

1960, You Learn by Living.

305. Daughters will be grateful and remember all their lives the things which their father introduced them to: gentleness and thoughtfulness and appreciation of themselves as women. These are qualities which, someday, they will look for in their maturity.

1960, You Learn by Living.

306. The mature person will admit, "It was my fault. The mistake was of my own making. Now that I understand why it happened, why I made the wrong choice, I'll try not to make the same mistake again."

1960, You Learn by Living.

307. You gain strength, courage and confidence by every experience in which you really stop to look fear in the face.

1960, You Learn by Living.

308. Freedom makes a huge requirement of every human being. With freedom comes responsibility. For the person who is unwilling to grow up, the person who does not want to carry his own weight, this is a frightening prospect.

1960, You Learn by Living.

309. Too many people have forgotten good manners and their importance in smoothing and making gracious and pleasant our dealings with our fellows. I am not referring now to rigid rules of etiquette but to the simple human kindness that is the foundation of all formal politeness.

1960, You Learn by Living.

310. Happiness is not a goal, it is a by-product. Paradoxically, the one sure way not to be happy is deliberately to map out a way of life in which one would please oneself completely and exclusively.

1960, You Learn by Living.

311. Unhappiness is an inward, not an outward, thing. It is as independent of circumstances as is happiness.

1960, You Learn by Living.

312. One of the most effective techniques in dealing with people is to appeal to them for their help. If they think you are in need of their assistance and that you will appreciate it, they are apt to do their best to help fill your need.

1960, You Learn by Living.

313. To force anything upon an individual is rarely successful in helping him develop his own individuality.

1960, You Learn by Living.

314. Nothing has ever been achieved by the person who says, "It can't be done."

1960, You Learn by Living.

315. Love and death come to us all, no matter what the circumstances of our lives. In the big things that matter, the similarities are far greater than the differences.

1960, You Learn by Living.

316. It is a brave thing to have the courage to be an individual; it is also, perhaps, a lonely thing. But it is better than not being an individual, which is to be nobody at all.

1960, You Learn by Living.

317. One of the secrets of using your time well is to gain a certain ability to maintain peace within yourself so that much can go on around you and you can stay calm inside.

1960, You Learn by Living.

318. An important part of self-knowledge is that it gives one a better realization of the inner strength that can be called upon, of which one may be quite unaware.

1960, You Learn by Living.

319. If you want a world ruled by law and not by force you must build up, from the very grassroots, a respect for law.
1960, You Learn by Living.

320. A leader must not get too far ahead or he will outdistance his followers; but he must move at least a step ahead.
1960, You Learn by Living.

321. Each new bit of knowledge, each new experience is an extra tool in meeting new problems and working them out.
1960, You Learn by Living.

322. I had to learn by doing and I believe I would never have learned had certain things not been forced upon me.
1960, You Learn by Living.

323. Nothing I have ever learned has failed to be useful to me at some time or other, often in the most unexpected way and in some quite unforeseen context.
1960, You Learn by Living.

324. The learning process must go on as long as we live.
1960, You Learn by Living.

325. There is no human being from whom we cannot learn something if we are interested enough to dig deep.
1960, You Learn by Living.

326. None of us can afford to stop learning or to check our curiosity about new things, or to lose our humility in the face of new situations.
1960, You Learn by Living.

327. You must be interested in anything that comes your way.

1960, You Learn by Living.

328. We can grow only as long as we are interested.

1960, You Learn by Living.

329. One thing life has taught me: if you are interested, you never have to look for new interests. They come to you. They will gravitate as automatically as the needle to the north.

1960, You Learn by Living.

330. A mature person is one who does not think only in absolutes, who is able to be objective even when deeply stirred emotionally, who has learned that there is both good and bad in all people and in all things, and who walks humbly and deals charitably with the circumstances of life, knowing that in this world all of us need both love and charity.

1960, You Learn by Living.

331. Self-pity and withdrawal from the battle are the beginning of misery.

1960, You Learn by Living.

332. It is the better part of wisdom to regard the mistake as experience which will help guide you in the future, a part, though a painful part, of your education. For all of us, no matter how good our training, will make bad choices. We will, through increased experience, make better choices as life goes on.

1960, You Learn by Living.

333. We hear a great deal about the need for self-expression but, by and large, it rarely brings the same returns in basic satisfaction that come with going beyond the self to meet another person's needs.

1960, You Learn by Living.

334. We cannot say, "Nothing has changed," or "The old ways were best." The point is that the old conditions are gone and we are left confronting the new.

1960, You Learn by Living.

335. The child who is aware that his parents do not tell him the truth will assume that the practical method is to lie. The child who sees his parents sacrifice everything for material possessions will not believe that spiritual values are important.

1960, You Learn by Living.

336. Until one sees with one's own eyes and comes to feel with one's own heart, one will never understand other people.

1960, You Learn by Living.

337. An important ingredient for the politician is the ability to attract and draw people to him. All political action is filtered through other human beings.

1960, You Learn by Living.

338. Politics is the participation of the citizen in his government. The kind of government he has depends entirely on the quality of that participation.

1960, You Learn by Living.

339. A good public servant becomes so at a high cost of personal sacrifice. We need such men; when we find them we owe them our gratitude and, above all, our respect.

1960, You Learn by Living.

340. It is difficult to give anyone a list of books which, in themselves, will provide him or her with a culture. What counts, in the long run, is not what you read; it is what you sift through your own mind; it is the ideas and impressions that are aroused in you by your reading. It is the ideas stirred in your own mind, the ideas which are a reflection of your own thinking, which make you an interesting person.

1960, You Learn by Living.

341. Readjustment is endless. Readjustment is a kind of private revolution. Each time you learn something new you must readjust the whole framework of your knowledge. It seems to me that one is forced to make inner and outer adjustments all one's life. The process never ends. And yet, for a great many people, this is a continuing problem because they appear to have an innate fear of change, no matter what form it takes. No matter how outwardly tranquil or unchanging one's situation may appear to be, it requires constant readjustment.

1960, You Learn by Living.

342. No relationship in this world ever remains warm and close unless a real effort is made on both sides to keep it so. Human relationships, like life itself, can never remain static. They grow or they diminish. But, in either case, they change. To be able to build new relations is as important as to hold the old ones, though sometimes one is obliged to sever old relationships.

1960, You Learn by Living.

343. Or, instead of love, perhaps the better word would be respect. That, I think, is a noble word, an indication of a certain attitude toward one's fellow men. Used too often in a subservient sense, it is more properly a token of equality.

1960, You Learn by Living.

344. It is possible that to feel respect for mankind is better than to feel love for it. Love can often be misguided and do as much harm as good, but respect can do only good. It assumes that the other person's stature is as large as one's own, his rights as reasonable, his needs as important.

1960, You Learn by Living.

345. Where your ideas are at a wide variance from those of others, there is no necessity, no advantage, in forcing your ideas down their throats. If you live steadfastly in accordance with them, you will eventually gain respect for your stand.

1960, You Learn by Living.

346. [. . .] It is often the people who refuse to assume any responsibility who are apt to be the sharpest critics of those who do.

1960, You Learn by Living.

347. Many people are as vigorous at sixty-five as they were at forty-five, with the added advantage of years of experience. Yet they often face compulsory retirement. If such people are wise they may arrange to go somewhere else, where their past experience is appreciated and where they can exercise the same profession.

1960, You Learn by Living.

348. [. . .] [My] satisfaction is not in politics, not in the interesting things I do. It is in being with people I am fond of

and feeling that in some small way I can make life happier and more interesting for them, or help them to achieve their objective. To me that is more important than anything else in my life.

1960, You Learn by Living.

349. Important as self-discipline is to a child, it is increasingly important as one grows older. Then it is really essential for your well-being to regulate your life and your habits in a sensible way.

1960, You Learn by Living.

350. Until you have been able to face the truth about yourself you cannot be really sympathetic or understanding in regard to what happens to other people.

1960, You Learn by Living.

351. Without self-respect, few people are able to feel genuine respect for others.

1960, You Learn by Living.

352. [...] Too little attention is paid to the passive sins, such as apathy and laziness, which in the long run can have a more devastating and destructive effect upon society than the others.

1960, You Learn by Living.

353. If you approach each new person you meet in a spirit of adventure you will find that you become increasingly interested in them and endlessly fascinated by the new channels of thought and experience and personality that you encounter. I don't mean simply the famous people of the world, but people from every walk and condition of life.

1960, You Learn by Living.

354. It's your life—but only if you make it so. The standards by which you live must be your own standards, your own values, your own conviction in regard to what is right and wrong, what is true and false, what is important and what is trivial. When you adopt the standards and the values of someone else or a community or a pressure group, you surrender your own integrity. You become, to the extent of your surrender, less of a human being.
1960, You Learn by Living.

355. Desperate men don't strike. During the depression there were few strikes. A strike is a sign of a worker's faith that he can better his condition.
1960, You Learn by Living.

356. [. . .] Being a success is tied up very closely with being one's own kind of individual.
1960, You Learn by Living.

357. Success must include two things: the development of an individual to his utmost potentiality and a contribution of some kind to one's world.
1960, You Learn by Living.

358. Unless time is good for something it is good for nothing.
1960, You Learn by Living.

359. The most unhappy people in the world are those who face the days without knowing what to do with their time.
1960, You Learn by Living.

360. [. . .] If you have more projects than you have time for, you are not going to be an unhappy person.
1960, You Learn by Living.

361. Learn to concentrate, to give all your attention to the thing at hand, and then to be able to put it aside and go on to the next thing without confusion.

1960, You Learn by Living.

362. Perhaps an important ingredient in timing is patience, an enormous amount of patience. A second ingredient in timing is clear awareness of the extent to which the people are with you.

1960, You Learn by Living.

363. Do not ask or expect to have anyone with you on everything. Do not try for it. To reach such a state of unanimity would mean that you would risk losing your own individuality to attain it.

1960, You Learn by Living.

364. I never can understand why so many people are afraid to live their own lives as they themselves think is right.

1960, You Learn by Living.

365. If you can develop this ability to see what you look at, to understand its meaning, to readjust your knowledge to this new information, you can continue to learn and to grow as long as you live and you'll have a wonderful time doing it.

1960, You Learn by Living.

366. To be useful is, in a way, to justify one's own existence.

1960, You Learn by Living.

367. Not to arrive at a clear understanding of one's own values is a tragic waste. You have missed the whole point of what life is for.

1960, You Learn by Living.

368. I have only two remedies for weariness: one is change and the other is relaxation.

>1960, You Learn by Living.

369. A woman is like a tea bag; you never know how strong it is until it's in hot water.

>1960, You Learn by Living.

370. Women have one advantage over men. Throughout history they have been forced to make adjustments. The result is that, in most cases, it is less difficult for a woman to adapt to new situations than it is for a man.

>1960, You Learn by Living.

371. Most women, I think, though they may complain a little about this, would agree that meeting the needs of others is not a real burden; it is what makes life worth living. It is probably the deepest satisfacion a woman has.

>1960, You Learn by Living.

372. Since everybody is an individual, nobody can be you. You are unique. No one can tell you how to use your time. It is yours. Your life is your own. You mold it. You make it.

>1960, You Learn by Living.

373. Our knowledge of human beings is limited. We cannot know all about any other human being. For the protection of society, if a human being seems dangerous we have a right to limit his contacts and thus protect others from the danger. But I doubt if we have a right to take away a gift which we alone cannot give. For that reason I believe the movement against capital punishment is growing stronger in our country. It is a good thing to have people think about the problem at this time. I hope many people will give it se-

rious reflection and come to the conclusion that I have—
that human beings have no right to take each other's lives.
March 14, 1960, "My Day."

374. The health of the future city dwellers and the health of
our whole country depends on providing young people
with an environment in which they can grow instead of de-
teriorating.
March 21, 1960, "My Day."

375. Above everything, we must insist that we learn to live
together in the future and that the primary aim of a nation
is no longer to learn to die for one's country. It is more difficult, but far more necessary, to learn to live for one's country.
February 27, 1961, "My Day."

376. Throughout our history, those who have wanted to
send their children to church schools or to private schools
have done so at their own expense. In point of fact, however, the great majority of our children have been educated
in the public schools.
March 6, 1961, "My Day."

377. When one is making these short speeches, climbing up
a ladder onto a sound truck and trying to speak above other
noises of passing traffic, I often wonder how much sense
one really makes.
August 30, 1961, "My Day."

378. Be flexible, but stick to your principles.
1962, Book of Common Sense Etiquette.

379. Though the circumstances of life shift rapidly and the
acknowledged leaders and arbiters have changed the rules

of behavior throughout the ages of man, the fundamental basis of good behavior in kindness and consideration for others has never changed.

1962, Book of Common Sense Etiquette.

380. True patriotism springs from a belief in the dignity of the individual, freedom and equality not only for Americans but for all people on earth, universal brotherhood and good will, and a constant and earnest striving toward the principles and ideals on which this country was founded.

1962, Book of Common Sense Etiquette.

381. There is no more precious experience in life than friendship. And I am not forgetting love and marriage as I write this; the lovers, or the man and wife, who are not friends are but weakly joined together. One enlarges his circle of friends through contact with many people. One who limits those contacts narrows the circle and frequently his own point of view as well.

1962, Book of Common Sense Etiquette.

382. If at all times the husband manages somehow to convey to his wife the impression that she is both his hostess and his guest, as well as his friend, loved one, companion, and partner in life, he will not go far wrong in his behavior to her.

1962, Book of Common Sense Etiquette.

383. How do you become the kind of human being with whom it is a privilege to associate? I have found that the secret lies in the willingness to listen to other people and in drawing from them through their experiences, through their conflicts and confusions, something that adds to your own understanding of human beings in general.

1962, Book of Common Sense Etiquette.

384. Success in marriage depends on being able when you get over being in love, to really love, [. . .] you never know anyone until you marry them.

1962, Book of Common Sense Etiquette.

385. I am sure that the number of unhappy marriages and divorces would decrease sharply if only the so common program of falling in love first and then learning to know each other were reversed.

1962, Book of Common Sense Etiquette.

386. The greatest tragedy of old age is the tendency for the old to feel unneeded, unwanted, and of no use to anyone; the secret of happiness in the declining years is to remain interested in life, as active as possible, useful to others, busy, and forward looking.

1962, Book of Common Sense Etiquette.

387. An American traveling abroad is an ambassador not only for the United States, but also for the concept of democracy and, if he is a white American, for the entire white race. Wherever he goes, America and democracy will be thought of with a little more or a little less respect after he has departed.

1962, Book of Common Sense Etiquette.

388. To have a friend who knows you by name gives you a sense that you are not alone in the world.

April 11, 1962, "My Day."

389. In the long run there is no more liberating, no more exhilarating experience than to determine one's position, state it bravely, and then act boldly.

1963, Tomorrow Is Now.

390. It is not too much to say that every bad situation is a result of apathy, of lack of planning, of individuals who think, "After all, it's not my business."

1963, Tomorrow Is Now.

391. The best in us is something we have to learn to control. It would be wise if we came to realize how it functions on so many different levels. Habit is one of the controlling factors.

1963, Tomorrow Is Now.

392. It has always been my conviction that example is the best evidence.

1963, Tomorrow Is Now.

393. Example is the best lesson there is.

1963, Tomorrow Is Now.

394. It is often possible to gain more real insight into human beings and their motivation by reading great fiction than by personal acquaintance.

1963, Tomorrow Is Now.

395. The answer to fear is not to cower and hide; it is not to surrender feebly without contest. The answer is to stand and face it boldly. Look at it, analyze it, and, in the end, act. With action, confidence grows.

1963, Tomorrow Is Now.

396. Our impact on the rest of the world is the sum total of what each of us does as a private citizen. We tell citizens in foreign lands what kind of people we are by what we do here.

1963, Tomorrow Is Now.

397. We face the future fortified only with the lessons we have learned from the past. It is today that we must create the world of the future.

1963, Tomorrow Is Now.

398. It is tragic to realize that the majority of human beings, even the so-called educated, call upon only the smallest fraction of their potential capacity.

1963, Tomorrow Is Now.

399. For the young person the discovery of his own unsuspected capacity is an exciting, a liberating experience. We cannot deny that we have failed dismally to achieve this result of helping our young people to develop their maximum capacity.

1963, Tomorrow Is Now.

400. Human resources are the most valuable assets the world has.

1963, Tomorrow Is Now.

401. What we must learn to do is to create unbreakable bonds between the sciences and the humanities.

1963, Tomorrow Is Now.

402. We must plan now—long-range, farsighted, bold planning to meet the great challenges of the future.

1963, Tomorrow Is Now.

403. Until we have helped raise the living standards of other peoples in the world to the point where they want, need, and can buy our products—and you can't do that to any people until they have been adequately fed—we will be unable to create new markets and inevitably, slowly or

quickly, our own standard of living will begin to falter and decline.

1963, Tomorrow Is Now.

404. Certainly we must face the evidence that the color of the skin does not regulate the superiority or inferiority of the individual.

1963, Tomorrow Is Now.

405. We take turns setting off greater and greater explosions, in the oldest and most futile form of international politics, the age-old struggle to maintain a balance of power. Continued tests of greater or less power can lead nowhere but to ultimate disaster.

1963, Tomorrow Is Now.

406. Poverty is like a giant infection which contaminates everything—we know that unless we can eradicate it by the use of all our new scientific and economic materials, it can in time destroy us.

1963, Tomorrow Is Now.

407. Our trouble is that we do not demand enough of the people who represent us.

1963, Tomorrow Is Now.

408. The reading of books should be a constant voyage of exploration, of adventure, of excitement. The habit of reading is man's bulwark against loneliness, his window opening on life, his unending delight. It is also an open door onto all the paths of knowledge and experience and beauty.

1963, Tomorrow Is Now.

409. I believe that, with proper education to enable us to master the secrets of science, with a strong sense of responsibility for our own actions, with a clear awareness that our future is linked with the welfare of the world as a whole, we may justly anticipate that the life of the next generation will be richer, more powerful, more rewarding than any we have ever known.

1963, Tomorrow Is Now.

410. There is a general awareness that for a decade we have been going through a scientific revolution. But what we have failed to grasp is that if you have a revolution in one area, it is bound to affect all the other areas.

1963, Tomorrow Is Now.

411. One thing is certain: in this modern world of ours we cannot afford to forget that what we do at home is important in relation to the rest of the world.

1963, Tomorrow Is Now.

412. The function of democratic living is not to lower standards but to raise those that have been too low.

1963, Tomorrow Is Now.

413. [. . .] We are being peculiarly shortsighted in underpaying the purveyors of education.

1963, Tomorrow Is Now.

414. The future is literally in our hands to mold as we like. But we cannot wait until tomorrow. That cannot be repeated often enough.

1963, Tomorrow Is Now.

415. Too often, we tend to expect too much of people to whom we have given no training.

1963, Tomorrow Is Now.

416. Our Bill of Rights is really the basis for the Universal Declaration of Human Rights but, as we know, we have not yet succeeded here at home in proving ourselves staunch advocates of civil liberties and equal rights for all human beings throughout the country. We must correct this situation if we are going to have something better than pure materialism to offer the world.

1963, Tomorrow Is Now.

417. It is not more vacation we need—it is more vocation.

1963, Tomorrow Is Now.

"My Day"

The following is a chronological ordering of a selection of Mrs. Roosevelt's distributed newspaper columns, syndicated by United Features Syndicate, Inc. Many of the quotations in this work are from these and her hundreds of other columns that were published from 1935 to 1962. Our resources list identifies the various editions of these and her other writings, the ideas of which are often as timely today as they were then. Several of the quotations in this book are seen here in their original context.

When especially seen relative to the time lines shown in this book, we see Mrs. Roosevelt was continually commenting on and sharing her experiences about the important current events of her time.

These articles represent some of the most popular of her many columns, such as selected by teachers, journalists, and historians, also referred to in documentaries, including the PBS Television series "American Experience."

1939

February 27 DAR Resignation

September 2 Invasion of Poland

July 13 Women and Employment

July 14 Prohibition

August 5 Women and Work

1940
February 9 Democratic National Committee

1941
December 8 Pearl Harbor

1943
July 14 Race Riots
August 13 Jews in Europe
October 15 Women in War

1945
April 21 Leaving the White House

1947
October 29 Hollywood and the House Un-American
     Activities Committee

1949
October 5 Navajo Indians

1954
April 16 H-Bomb
May 14 Equal Rights
May 20 Brown vs. Board of Education

1955
May 13 Women and Population
October 17 Housewives

1957

May 24 Desegregation

December 2 Apartheid

1958

November 5 Television

1960

March 26 Sit-ins

April 11 Civil Rights Bill

October 21 First Lady

1961

May 8 Space

December 10 Cold War

1962

February 16 Commission on the Status of Women

DAR Resignation

WASHINGTON, FEBRUARY 27, 1939—I am having a peaceful day. I drove my car a short distance out of the city this morning to pilot some friends of mine who are starting off for a vacation in Florida. I think this will be my only excursion out of the White House today, for I have plenty of work to do on an accumulation of mail, and I hope to get through in time to enjoy an evening of uninterrupted reading. I have been debating in my mind for some time, a question which I have had to debate with myself once or twice before in my life. Usually I have decided differently from the way in which I am deciding now. The question is, if you belong to an organization and disapprove of an action which is typical of a policy, should you resign or is it better to work for a changed point of view within the organization? In the past, when I was able to work actively in any organization to which I belonged, I have usually stayed until I had at least made a fight and had been defeated.

Even then, I have, as a rule, accepted my defeat and decided I was wrong or, perhaps, a little too far ahead of the thinking for the majority at that time. I have often found that the thing in which I was interested was done some years later. But in this case, I belong to an organization in which I can do no active work. They have taken an action which has been widely talked of in the press. To remain as a member implies approval of that action, and therefore I am resigning.

Invasion of Poland

HYDE PARK, SEPTEMBER 2, 1939—At 5 o'clock this morning, our telephone rang and it was the President in Washington to tell me the sad news that Germany had invaded Poland and that her planes were bombing Polish cities. He told me that Hitler was about to address the Reichstag, so we turned on the radio and listened until 6 o'clock. Curiously enough, I had received a letter on my return last evening from a German friend who roomed with me in school in England. In this letter she said that when hate was rampant in the world, it was easy to believe harm of any nation, that she knew all the nations believed things that were not true about Germany, did not understand her position, and therefore hated her. She begged that we try to see Germany's point of view and not to judge her harshly.

As I listened to Hitler's speech, this letter kept returning to my mind. How can you feel kindly toward a man who tells you that German minorities have been brutally treated, first in Czechoslovakia and then in Danzig, but that never can Germany be accused of being unfair to a minority? I have seen evidence with my own eyes of what this same man has done to people belonging to a minority group—not only Jews, but Christians, who have long been German citizens.

Can one help but question his integrity? His knowledge of history seems somewhat sketchy too, for, after all, Poland possessed Danzig many years prior to the time that it ever belonged to Germany. And how can you say that you do not intend to make war on women and children and then send planes to bomb cities?

No, I feel no bitterness against the German people. I am deeply sorry for them, as I am for the people of all other European nations facing this horrible crisis. But for the man who has taken this responsibility upon his shoulders I can feel little pity. It is hard to see how he can sleep at night and think of the people in many nations whom he may send to their deaths.

Women and Employment

HYDE PARK, JULY 13, 1939—Yesterday, with great interest, I read Mrs. Carrie Chapman Catt's appeal to the National Federation of Business and Professional Women's Clubs. It seems to me so obvious that married women should not be discriminated against, that I cannot imagine anyone who would really consider such a proposition. It seems this discussion was given impetus by a rule in the federal government during the Depression, forbidding two married people to hold government positions. Now that the emergency is over, that rule has been rescinded, but there is, I think, one consideration in government employment that does not exist in private employment. The government wants to prevent the building up of a family bureaucracy.

It seems to me that if a generous sum is set, on which an adequate standard of living may be preserved for the average family that it might be well, if one member of the family earns that amount, to bar the employment of any other member of the family in government service. If a man and his wife together earn that amount, children who live in the same household should be barred from government employment. Such a rule would not be directed at women particularly, married or single, but, if adopted by the federal government, it should be very carefully considered for the same pattern might easily be followed by state and local governments.

I see by the morning papers that the Senate Committee has voted for delay on neutrality. One vote makes this important decision. These gentlemen must go on the theory that if you delay making up your mind long enough, perhaps you may never have to, for somebody else may make it up for you. My own experience is that the things you refuse to meet today always come back at you later on, usually under circumstances which make the decision twice as difficult as it originally was. I would not weep over the difficulties of the gentlemen who made this decision, were it not for the fact that the results of their decision may not rest on their heads alone but may affect innocent people in our country and other countries.

Prohibition

NEW YORK, JULY 14, 1939—A number of letters have come to me complaining bitterly about the fact that I said in an article recently that the repeal of Prohibition had been a crusade carried on by women. I know quite well, of course that the Democratic Party took the stand in its platform that Prohibition should be repealed. I have always felt, however, that the women's organization for repeal, which was a nonpartisan organization, laid the groundwork which finally brought about the vote for repeal.

I was one of those who was very happy when the original prohibition amendment passed. I thought innocently that a law in this country would automatically be complied with, and my own observation led me to feel rather ardently that the less strong liquor anyone consumed the better it was. During prohibition I observed the law meticulously, but I came gradually to see that laws are only observed with the consent of the individuals concerned and a moral change still depends on the individual and not on the passage of any law.

Little by little it dawned upon me that this law was not making people drink any less, but it was making hypocrites and law breakers of a great number of people. It seemed to me best to go back to the old situation in which, if a man or woman drank to excess, they were injuring themselves and their immediate family and friends and the act was a violation against their own sense of morality and no violation against the law of the land. I could never quite bring myself to work for repeal, but I could not oppose it, for intellectually I had to agree that it was the honest thing to do. My contacts are wide and I see a great many different groups of people, and I cannot say that I find that the change in the law has made any great change in conditions among young or old in the country today.

Women and Work

HYDE PARK, AUGUST 5, 1939—The other day I was sent a most amusing page from a magazine called "Future: The Magazine for Young Men." An article by Dr. S. N. Stevens, which contains the following quotation, was marked for my attention:

"Women are generally more intuitive than empirical. In other words, they play hunches instead of examining facts in the evaluation of a situation. And I have never yet seen one who, in a tight spot, didn't try to take advantage of the fact that she was a woman."

I am willing to agree to the first part of the paragraph, women have so much intuition and are so much quicker to feel things than men are that they occasionally count too much on that particular gift. However, the woman who has trained herself has the advantage over a man in that she still has her intuition, but to it she has added his gift of examining facts and evaluating all the factors entering into a situation. As to the second half of his statement, I'll grant some women do it, but they are never the women who succeed in their jobs. They are the ones who always preyed on men and always will, for that is a job in itself.

There are so many occasions when a woman is in a tight spot which only she herself can face, that it is rather rare to find her trying to share her burden or ask for assistance on the ground that she is a woman.

What good would it do to try to get someone else to stand by when you are about to have a baby? What good would it do to turn to anyone else if your husband drank and you had to try to collect his wages before they were all spent? A woman may use her womanly wiles to help her in tight spots, but she isn't trading on being a woman, she is just handling the job which is hers, and frequently it is the job of handling a man and making him think he isn't being handled. These doctors and editors who write for magazines like this are very clever, but they should know a little more about women and real life before they venture to write about them.

Democratic National Committee

BOSTON, FEBRUARY 9, 1940—The members of the Democratic National Committee, who were meeting in Washington, came to tea. The ladies seemed particularly elated by the passage of a resolution which is a new milestone in the participation of women in party politics.

Steps of this kind are not of interest only to the women in one political party, they are of interest to all women, because what is done by one party is soon done also by the others. Those of us who believe that women's advice and influence are of importance in public affairs, look back with considerable interest at the record of our own party. In both major parties, the record shows the growing importance of women. I belong to the Democratic party, and so I give you my party's record here.

In 1919 the Executive Committee of the National Democratic Committee, anticipating the ratification of the constitutional amendment permitting women to vote, decided on September 27th, to admit women to membership. In 1920 Miss Charl Ormond Williams was elected vice chairman of the National Democratic Committee. In 1936, at the Democratic National Convention held in Philadelphia, women were named as alternates to the platform committee for the first time, with the privilege of voting when regular members were not present and now, on February 5, 1940, the Democratic National Committee meeting in Washington, has passed the following resolution:

"Whereas, it is the sense of this committee that women be given an equal voice in the affairs of the Democratic party."

"Now, therefore, be it resolved, that this committee recommend to the next Democratic National Convention a consideration of a resolution there to be introduced, providing that each State, District and Territory shall name two members to serve on the committee on platform and resolutions, and that the members so designated by each State, District and Territory shall be of the opposite sex."

In addition, resolutions passed provided that four delegates-at-large be chosen from each State for each Senator in Congress and it was recommended to the States that one-half of those delegates be women.

At present, in the Democratic party, women have fifty-fifty representation on the state committees in 38 States. Only 9 states in the Union do not give women equal representation on some of the political committees, either by party regulations or by law. Even more important than these gains, however, is the caliber of women chosen for political offices. I hope that every woman is going to feel a great responsibility, not only in holding party offices, but in choosing those who are to hold these offices and who will, therefore, represent the women of their communities.

Pearl Harbor

WASHINGTON, DECEMBER 8, 1941—I was going out in the hall to say goodbye to our cousins, Mr. and Mrs. Frederick Adams, and their children, after luncheon, and, as I stepped out of my room, I knew something had happened. All the secretaries were there, two telephones were in use, the senior military aides were on their way with messages. I said nothing because the words I heard over the telephone were quite sufficient to tell me that, finally, the blow had fallen, and we had been attacked.

Attacked in the Philippines, in Hawaii, and on the ocean between San Francisco and Hawaii. Our people had been killed not suspecting there was an enemy, who attacked in the usual ruthless way which Hitler has prepared us to suspect.

Because our nation has lived up to the rules of civilization, it will probably take us a few days to catch up with our enemy, but no one in this country will doubt the ultimate outcome. None of us can help but regret the choice which Japan has made, but having made it, she has taken on a coalition of enemies she must underestimate unless she believes we have sadly deteriorated since our first ships sailed into her harbor.

The clouds of uncertainty and anxiety have been hanging over us for a long time. Now we know where we are. The work for those who are at home seems to be obvious. First, to do our own job, whatever it is, as well as we can possibly do it. Second, to add to it everything we can do in the way of civilian defense. Now, at last, every community, must go to work to build up protection from attack.

We must build up the best possible community services, so that all of our people may feel secure because they know we are standing together and that whatever problems have to be met will be met by the community and not one lone individual. There is no weakness and insecurity when once this is understood.

Race Riots

FRANKTOWN, NEVADA, JULY 14, 1943—Some days ago, as the newspapers have recorded, I came to spend a few days in this beautiful valley. There are farms around us settled long ago by some hardy Swiss pioneers. Gurgling streams run down even now from the Mountains. Wildflowers bloom in the meadows, the pine trees and cottonwoods give you shade.

I have walked in the early mornings with the sun coming up, and again in the evening under the moon and watched the stars come out, and renewed my understanding of our pioneers who gave us this vast land of ours. They had no fear of new adventure, there was no pattern to follow in their lives, they accepted men as they proved themselves in the daily business of meeting emergencies.

Have we lost this spirit, do we fear to face the fact that we have new frontiers to conquer? I was sick at heart when I came here, over race riots which put us on a par with Nazism which we fight and make one tremble for what human beings may do when they no longer think but let themselves be dominated by their worst emotions. We are a mixed nation of many peoples and many religions, but most of us would accept the life of Christ as a pattern for our democratic way of life, and Christ taught love and never hate. We cannot settle strikes by refusing to understand their causes; we cannot prepare for a peaceful world unless we give proof of self-restraint, of open mindedness, of courage to do right at home, even if it means changing our traditional thinking and, for some of us, a sacrifice of our material interests.

Jews in Europe

HYDE PARK, AUGUST 13, 1943—I talked a little while yesterday morning with a representative from the group which is trying to formulate plans to save the Jewish people in Europe. Some people think of the Jewish people as a race. Others think of them purely as a religious group. But in Europe the hardships and persecution which they have had to endure for the past few years, have tended to bring them together in a group which identifies itself with every similar group, regardless whether it is religious or racial. The Jews are like all the other people of the world. There are able people among them, there are courageous people among them, there are people of extraordinary intellectual ability along many lines. There are people of extraordinary integrity and people of great beauty and great charm.

On the other hand, largely because of environment and economic conditions, there are people among them who cringe, who are dishonest, who try to take advantage of their neighbors, who are aggressive and unattractive. In other words, they are a cross-section of the human race, just as is every other nationality and every other religious group. But good or bad, they have suffered in Europe as has no other group. The percentage killed among them in the past few years far exceeds the losses among any of the United Nations in the battles which have been fought throughout the war.

Many of them for generations considered Germany, Poland, Rumania, and France their country and permanent home. It seems to me that it is in the part of common sense for the world as a whole to protest in its own interest against wholesale persecution, because none of us by ourselves would be strong enough to stand against a big enough group which decided to treat us in the same way. We may have our individual likes and dislikes, but this is a question which far transcends prejudices or inclinations.

It means the right of survival of human beings and their right to grow and improve. You and I may be hated by our neighbors, but if we know about it we try to change the things within us which brought it about. That is the way civilized people develop; murder and annihilation are never a satisfactory answer for the few who escape grow up more bitter against their persecutors, and a day of reckoning always comes, which is what the story of Moses in the bulrushes teaches us.

I do not know what we can do to save the Jews in Europe and to find them homes, but I know that we will be the sufferers if we let great wrongs occur without exerting ourselves to correct them.

Women in War

WASHINGTON, OCTOBER 15, 1943—The film which we saw last night was the story of the British Women's Military Auxiliary Services, and it was one of the most thrilling stories I have seen on the screen.

By and large, I am not sure the men of the United States are encouraging their wives and daughters to go into our auxiliary military services. I am not even sure our women are convinced they are needed in these services. They may wonder whether they really would free a man to do a job which they cannot do.

I realize, of course, that our WACS, WAVES, Marines and Spars are not being trained for as great a variety of activities as the British women are. That makes the service less interesting. In addition, they probably resent the restrictions put upon them as to the places where they are to be allowed to work.

If I were young enough, I would rather be a nurse in the Army or Navy, for they are allowed to share more nearly the men's existence. They know that there will be no attitude on the part of the boys which says "Oh yes, you have come in to wear a uniform, but you don't really mean ever to do a job which will inconvenience you or change the ease we men are expected to provide for our women."

Life in the armed services is hard and uncomfortable, but I think women can stand up under that type of living just as well as men. It made me unhappy last night to see what the British women are doing and then to remember certain speeches I have read by gentlemen who oppose women's full participation in the auxiliary military services, when there is so much they could do. Why should British, Australian and New Zealand women render services to and with our men and we be barred?

Leaving the White House

WASHINGTON, APRIL 21, 1945—There is always a certain emotional strain about the last time for anything. When you have lived twelve years in a house, even though you have always known that it belonged to the nation, you grow fond of the house itself, and fonder still of all the people connected with your life in that house.

Yesterday the President and Mrs. Truman and Miss Truman lunched here with us and, from then on, I began to do "last things." At four o'clock, I greeted the members of my press conference for the last time. I have always looked out at the Washington Monument from my bedroom window the last thing at night, and the little red light at the top of it has twinkled at me in friendly fashion. That simple shaft, so tall and straight, has often made me feel during this war that, if Washington could be steadfast through Valley Forge, we could be steadfast today in spite of anxiety and sorrow.

Now, I have spent my last night in the White House. I have had my last breakfast on the sun porch. And all today, I shall be saying goodbye to different people who have been loyal and kind and have given all that they could for the success of my husband's Administration or for the comfort and welfare of us all as a family. Yet I cannot feel that it is goodbye for, when you are fond of people, you are sure to meet again.

I wonder if others have been thinking, as I have, of the rather remarkable way in which our people and our government have passed through this major period of change. Ordinarily, when there is a change of administration, there is a period between election and inauguration during which the outgoing president and his family prepare for their departure, while the incoming President and his family prepare to assume their new responsibilities.

Never before has a sudden change of presidents come about during a war. Yet, from the time that Mr. Truman, followed closely by Secretary of State Stettinius, walked into my sitting room and I told them of my husband's death, everything has moved in orderly fashion. There was consternation and grief but, at the same time, courage and confidence in the ability of this country and its people to back new leaders and to carry through the objectives to which the people have pledged themselves.

That this attitude established itself so quickly is a tribute to President Truman, to the members of the Cabinet, and to the Congress. But above all, it is a tribute to the people as a whole and it reaffirms our confidence in the future.

Hollywood and the House Un-American Activities Committee

NEW YORK, OCTOBER 29, 1947—I have waited a while before saying anything about the Un-American Activities Committee's current investigation of the Hollywood film industry. I would not be very much surprised if some writers or actors or stagehands, or what not, were found to have Communist leanings, but I was surprised to find that, at the start of the inquiry, some of the big producers were so chicken-hearted about speaking up for the freedom of their industry.

One thing is sure—none of the arts flourishes on censorship and repression. And by this time it should be evident that the American public is capable of doing its own censoring. Certainly, the Thomas Committee is growing more ludicrous daily. The picture of six officers ejecting a writer from the witness stand because he refused to say whether he was a Communist or not is pretty funny, and I think before long we are all going to see how hysterical and foolish we have become.

The film industry is a great industry with infinite possibilities for good and bad. Its primary purpose is to entertain people. On the side, it can do many other things. It can popularize certain ideals, it can make education palatable. But in the long run, the judge who decides whether what it does is good or bad is the man or woman who attends the movies. In a democratic country I do not think the public will tolerate a removal of its right to decide what it thinks of the ideas and performances of those who make the movie industry work.

I have never liked the idea of an Un-American Activities Committee. I have always thought that a strong democracy should stand by its fundamental beliefs and that a citizen of the United States should be considered innocent until he is proved guilty.

If he is employed in a government position where he has access to secret and important papers, then for the sake of security he must undergo some special tests. However, I doubt whether the loyalty test really adds much to our safety, since no Communist would hesitate to sign it and he would be in good standing until he was proved guilty. So it seems to me that we might as well do away with a test which is almost an insult to any loyal American citizen.

What is going on in the Un-American Activities Committee worries me primarily because little people have become frightened and we find ourselves living in the atmosphere of a police state, where people close doors before they state what they think or look over their shoulders apprehensively before they express an opinion.

I have been one of those who have carried the fight for complete freedom of information in the United Nations. And while accepting the fact that some of our press, our radio commentators, our prominent citizens and our movies may at times be blamed legitimately for things they have said and done, still I feel that the fundamental right of freedom of thought and expression is essential. If you curtail what the other fellow says and does, you curtail what you yourself may say and do.

In our country we must trust the people to hear and see both the good and the bad and to choose the good. The Un-American Activities Committee seems to me to be better for a police state than for the USA.

Navajo Indians

NEW YORK, OCTOBER 5, 1949—One of the Soviet attacks on the democracies, particularly the United States, centers on our racial policies. In recent months the Russians have been particularly watching our attitude toward the native Indians of our country. So, the question of what we do about our Indians, important as it used to be for the sake of justice, is enhanced in importance now because it is part of the fight which we and other democracies must wage, day in and day out, in perfecting our governmental household so that it will not be vulnerable to attack by the Communists.

For that reason our country as a whole should understand what is going on at the present time in Congress in this connection. This particular little plot, shall I call it, has to do with the Navajo and Hopi. There are 11 Hopi pueblos, surrounded by Navajo country. The Navajo number about 65,000 and are the largest Indian tribe north of Mexico. The Hopi represent the most perfect flowering of pre-Columbian culture from the Rio Grande to the Arctic.

For purposes largely of publicity, because it was not really necessary, the Interior Department drafted a bill to authorize a rehabilitation program. This bill re-authorized already-authorized appropriations, and the interested public and the Indians gained an impression that the bill actually appropriated $90,000,000 for their needs. It did nothing of the kind. The hope was that it would create public interest and thus stir the appropriations committee in Congress to appropriate some very much needed money. The bill was approved by voice votes in the House and the Senate and sent to President Truman. Even if it is signed by the

President, funds must still be appropriated to put the bill into effect.

I certainly hope President Truman will veto this bill. One provision of it would place all Navajo and Hopi Indians under the state laws of Arizona, Utah, New Mexico and Colorado. Only a few minor exceptions in the matter of land law and property taxation were made; nothing was said of water rights; and without any exceptions the Navajo and the Hopi are placed under the jurisdiction of the state and local courts.

For a hundred years it has been the U.S. policy to allow Indians their own tribal, customary law. Under Section 9 of this new bill we will interfere with all the things that are important to them—their religion, their art, their self-governing arrangements. The very things that those who study Indian life consider most important, this bill would destroy.

There is a constant effort going on to transfer Indian property to whites, and one of the most successful ways in the past has been to disrupt the Indian social system. Between 1887 and 1933, through land allotments, we transferred 90 million acres of the best Indian land to whites. This was largely done by the method of persuading or compelling the individualization of tribal properties.

In 1934, under the Indian Reorganization Act, land allotments were stopped. Now there is still another bill up for consideration, called the Butler-D'Ewart Bill. This authorizes any Indian individual, if declared competent, to sell his equity regardless of the consent of the co-owners and, of course, strikes a body blow at all Indian corporate holdings.

The intent is similar to the Indian Omnibus Bill of 1923 which Albert D. Fall nearly succeeded in getting enacted.

There are many other things that are being done in Congress at the present time and which the public knows little or nothing about.

Often the Indians themselves and the welfare groups that are trying to watch legislation for them know nothing about what is being done by the conferees in Congress.

Are we indifferent to the way our Indians are treated? If not, we had better let our representatives in Congress know that we do not like the present trend of legislation.

H-Bomb

NEW YORK, APRIL 16, 1954—Increasingly, people are talking to me about the new H-bomb and its dangers. Even on "Meet the Press" I was asked if the knowledge that one could carry a devastating bomb in a suitcase didn't frighten me, and so I have decided to tell you what I feel about this whole situation.

It seems to me that the discovery of this latest bomb has actually outlawed the use of atomic bombs. The power of destruction is so great that unless we face the fact that no one in the world can possibly use it and therefore it must be outlawed as a weapon, we risk putting an end to all civilization. However, this realization makes it necessary to think of other things much more critically.

The day that we agree the world over that no one can use an atom bomb, we must either agree immediately on total disarmament, except for a united force in the United Nations, or we must make sure that we have better weapons than anyone else. We must have the best of the less destructive weapons, such as tanks, guns, etc. We are not equal as to population with the Communist world.

Therefore, the free world must stand together to defend itself. It will not do to rely on a weapon that we cannot use for protection. It is entirely obvious that were we, because we had no other strength, to use the H-bomb, let us say against an enemy that seemed to threaten us or that seemed to threaten the security of an area of the world that we felt should not fall to Soviet domination, instead of having the sympathy of the world we would, by that one action, have created fear and hatred of us.

No one can use this new destructive weapon without destroying innumerable innocent people. It would not be only our enemies that would condemn us, it would be our own conscience.

The conscience of America is a very real thing and if, because of any temptation whatsoever, we use this terrific weapon first, there are few of us in this country who could live with our own conscience.

Before we drift into war in one way or another, I feel that every possible agency, primarily the United Nations and its negotiation machinery, should be called into play. Sometimes I think we rely too much on negotiation only among the great powers. True, there is no force set up in the United Nations and you cannot rely on the enforcement of peace through an already set-up compulsory force provided by every member nation in the United Nations.

Just because of this, however, the mobilization of world opinion and methods of negotiation should be developed and used by every nation in order to strengthen the United Nations. Then if we are forced into war, it will be because there has been no way to prevent it through negotiation and the mobilization of world opinion. In which case we should have the voluntary support of many nations, which is far better than the decision of one nation alone, or even of a few nations.

I dislike fear and I confess to being on the whole rather free from it. But not to look at the dangers of the present and make up our minds that we do not want to drift, but that we want to use all the machinery there is to prevent war, seems to me foolhardy.

I think the women of this country, if they face the fact of the present situation, will agree with me that this is a time for action—not for war, but for mobilization of every bit of peace machinery. It is also a time for facing the fact that you cannot use a weapon, even though it is the weapon that gives you greater strength than other nations, if it is so destructive that it practically wipes out large areas of land and great numbers of innocent people.

Equal Rights

HYDE PARK, MAY 14, 1954—I have been getting a good many letters of late about the Equal Rights amendment, which has been reported out favorably to the House by the House Judiciary Committee. Some of the women who write me seem to think that if this amendment is passed there will be no further possibility of discrimination against women. They feel that the time has come to declare that women shall be treated in all things on an equal basis with men. I hardly think it is necessary to declare this, since as a theory it is fairly well accepted today by both men and women. But in practice it is not accepted, and I doubt very much whether it ever will be.

Other women of my acquaintance are writing me in great anxiety, for they are afraid that the dangers of the amendment are not being properly considered. The majority of these women are employed in the industrial field. Their fear is that labor standards safeguarded in the past by legislation will be wrecked, and that the amendment will curtail and impair for all time the powers of both state and federal government to enact any legislation that may be necessary and desirable to protect the health and safety of women in industry. I do not know which group is right, but I feel that if we work to remove from our statute books those laws which discriminate against women today we might accomplish more and do it in a shorter time than will be possible through the passage of this amendment.

Brown vs. Board of Education

NEW YORK, MAY 20, 1954—While I was on the "Tex and Jinx [television] Show" I was given the news of the unanimous Supreme Court decision that wiped out segregation in the schools. I am delighted this was a unanimous decision because I think it will be difficult for the states with segregated school systems to hold out against such a ruling.

If it were not for the fact that segregation in itself means inequality, the old rule of giving equal facilities might have gone on satisfying our sense of justice for a long time. It is very difficult, however, to ensure real equality under a segregated system, and the mere fact that you cannot move freely anywhere in your country and be as acceptable everywhere as your neighbor creates an inequality.

Southerners always bring up the question of marriage between the races, and I realize that that is the question of real concern to people. But it seems to me a very personal question which must be settled by family environment and by the development of the cultural and social patterns within a country. One can no longer lay down rules as to what individuals will do in any area of their lives in a world that is changing as fast as ours is changing today.

Women and Population

NEW YORK, MAY 13, 1955—Few people may have noticed a little item in the newspapers the other day under a dateline from Washington. The Population Reference Bureau says that since 1900 the proportion of persons over 65 has doubled from four to eight percent. There also has been a steady increase in the proportion of women, particularly in the age groups above 20.

In terms of voting power, ownership of land and corporate equities the United States could be seen on the road toward a gerontomatriarchy—"control by aging females," the bureau said.

This will make us smile, particularly in a country where for so many years women were scarce and the young man held the important position in our population.

This fact, however, should give us a little food for thought. Why do women live longer than men? They are the "weaker" sex, they bear the children and, therefore, should wear out more quickly since we no longer live in a time when men must run the daily risks of hunting for their food and having to defend by physical prowess their homes on a day-by-day basis.

Is the answer perhaps that women, through the ages, have had to learn how to conserve their strength and to build resistance?

More and more in the modern world men have been obliged to set their goal for success in a competitive atmosphere. One may be under as great a strain when sitting quietly at a desk as in the days when one went out hunting to sustain himself. So, since men must work every minute in order to excel and must work at high tension in constant competition with all those around him, men often die earlier than do women.

The modern killers are heart disease and cancer and brain hemorrhage—all of which represent the pace at which modern man lives. Transportation and communication have so greatly increased in speed that man can cover more ground and do more than he could in years gone by, yet he stood up better apparently under hard physical labor than seems to be the case under the modern type of strain.

I wonder if there is not something in teaching children how to acquire an inner calm. It seems to me that in some of the books written in days gone by there was more emphasis on serenity. It may be that we must learn how to have inner serenity in spite of outward speed and activity.

Certainly, we should find ways of keeping a better balance in our population, for whether in youth or in age I think too great a predominance of one or the other sex is a distinct drawback. Our doctors had better start finding out why men wear out faster than women and they had better keep them alive for the happiness and contentment of all.

Housewives

NEW YORK, OCTOBER 17, 1955—Recently I received a letter which raised a question of interest to many women. It reads as follows:

"Reading your article in the August Safeway Magazine gives me the inspiration and opportunity I have long been looking for, namely to 'speak' to you regarding the word 'housewife,' used to define the greatest profession we women perform.

QUESTION: What is your occupation?
ANSWER: Housewife, wife of a house.
QUESTIONING A CHILD: What does your father do?
ANSWER: He is a lawyer on Wall Street, N.Y.C.
QUESTION: What is your mother's occupation?
ANSWER: Oh, she is just a housewife.

"I have heard this on TV. I am sure other women have cringed at the term. The dictionary defines the word as 'the woman in charge of a household.' 'Wife' is defined as 'a woman joined in marriage to a man as husband.'

"Surely there is another name for us. How do you feel about it? Why not write an article which will bring opinions from other married women?"

I must confess that in days gone by I have often entered myself on questionnaires as "housewife" without feeling the slightest embarrassment. Now I put down " writer" or "lecturer," because the major part of my life is taken up in this way rather than in running a home and watching over the daily needs of a household and children plus guests, as it used to be in earlier days. I am not sure, however, that I did not feel more useful when I had to be home the greater part of the time. I had to make very careful plans when I left home so that all would go on in the same way while I was gone. I was limited in my free time. One could never be sure that there would not be sudden illness which would make a change in plans inevitable, or that home tasks would not clash with some demands outside my family— and of course, the demands outside the family were always secondary.

Those were the days when on a questionnaire I would put down "housewife" and feel very proud of it, and I am quite sure that no woman has any reason for feeling humiliated by the title. It is one of the most skilled professions in the world. When one adds to the business of running a house the care and bringing up of children, there is so much needed preparation for this occupation that I think it could be classed today among the most skilled occupations in the world. To be sure, there are good and bad homes; and there are children who are well brought up and children who are badly brought up. This happens in any business or professional activity. But when one adds up what it means to a nation, one must concede that the well-run home and the well-brought-up children are much more important even than a well-run business. More people are affected by the occupation of a housewife and mother than are ever touched by any single business, no matter how large it may be.

Desegregation

HOUSTON, TEXAS, MAY 24, 1957—I am in Texas for two lectures on behalf of Bonds for Israel and arrived in Houston when a court hearing was being held on the speed for compliance with the Supreme Court's order on desegregation of schools.

This led the press to ask me a number of questions which, as a guest, I felt it was unfortunate for me to have to answer, particularly since I feel that my attitude and beliefs on this question have been so well known.

I was glad, however, to be able to express my strong feelings against violence in this issue anywhere in our country. And so I regret the decision made in Texas against the National Association for the Advancement of Colored People, for it seems to take away the right to use legal action to enforce the desegregation decision and, in a way, makes it more difficult to prevent violence.

I hope that I am wrong and that we will see a continuation of the staunchness shown by the citizens in Montgomery, Ala., who under the leadership of the Rev. Martin Luther King have adhered to nonviolence.

But human beings have a breaking point if denied an outlet for their emotions and convictions. Then violence may seem to be the only answer, and that hurts us, both at home and abroad.

Apartheid

NEW YORK, DECEMBER 2, 1957—People all over the world have been asked to sign a Declaration of Conscience to observe a day of protest against South Africa's apartheid policy. An international committee, composed of more than 150 world leaders from more than 43 nations, has designated Human Rights Day, December 10, as this worldwide day of protest. Particularly in India and in Africa, as well as in many other countries of the world, there will be demonstrations protesting the policy which is felt to be harmful to human relations the world over. Therefore it cannot be the domestic concern of one nation only, but of all nations.

More than 20 American communities have already said they would hold similar meetings. The Very Rev. James A. Pike is the U.S. national chairman and Rev. Martin Luther King, Jr. is the vice president of the committee in this country. The list of those who have signed the Declaration of Conscience is composed of the names of men all over the world who are known to have stood for equal rights for all human beings. It is true that there are peoples who are not as advanced as others, but as a rule this is due to lack of opportunity and can be corrected in one or two generations by education and environment.

When I was asked to sign this Declaration of Conscience, I at first hesitated. I felt that a country which needed to look at its own situation and acknowledge the basic rights of all its own citizens and work for the necessary changes which would bring every citizen in the United States the opportunity for complete development of his powers might better perhaps first sign a Declaration of Conscience covering his own country. I signed, however, because the situation here, bad as it is, is not quite the same as the situation in South Africa. The Negroes of our South have good leaders and though their education has been insufficient and their opportunities for advancement certainly not equal, still they have begun their upward climb. They are able to do much for themselves, and on the whole in this country there is a vast majority of people who are ready and willing to help them achieve equality of opportunity in every area of our complicated civilization.

Bitter as the feeling is at present in the South and in spite of the fact that communications between the races in many Southern states seem to have deteriorated, the Supreme Court decision and the feeling of the majority of the people of the nation will eventually, I am sure, bring about a solution to the present difficult situation. Someone suggested to me the other day that it might be started in the South by dividing boys' schools and girls' schools and putting all boys without discrimination into one school and all girls without discrimination into another, which would remove one of the chief objections of the Southerners. Whether this would help or not, I don't know. But I am confident that the pressure of the majority feeling in this nation will be so overwhelming for equal rights for all our citizens that sooner or later this problem must have a solution which satisfactorily safeguards these rights.

Television

NOVEMBER 5, 1958—If the use of leisure time is confined to looking at TV for a few extra hours every day, we will deteriorate as a people.

Actually, preparation for the use of leisure time should begin with our schoolchildren. The appreciation of many things in which we are not proficient ourselves but which we have learned to enjoy is one of the important things to cultivate in modern education. The arts in every field—music, drama, sculpture, painting—we can learn to appreciate and enjoy. We need not be artists, but we should be able to appreciate the work of artists. Crafts of every kind, the value of things made by hand, by skilled people who love to work with wood or clay or stone will develop taste in our people.

These are all things that can give us joy and many of us will find that we are capable of acquiring a certain amount of skill we never dreamed we had, which will give an outlet to a creative urge. But these things must be taught, and in the age now developing about us they are important things. For if man is to be liberated to enjoy more leisure, he must also be prepared to enjoy this leisure fully and creatively.

For people to have more time to read, to take part in their civic obligations, to know more about how their government functions and who their officials are might mean in a democracy a great improvement in the democratic processes. Let's begin, then, to think how we can prepare old and young for these new opportunities. Let's not wait until they come upon us suddenly and we have a crisis that we will be ill prepared to meet.

Sit-ins

HYDE PARK, MARCH 26, 1960—We have all been very much upset by the situation in South Africa. But equally upsetting has been the news from Alabama, where nine college students were expelled from school for their sit-down strike. A visitor came to tell me that when a sympathy strike was attempted on behalf of these students, the police set up gun posts around the college campus, tapped the telephone lines to the church where meetings were being held, and altogether created an atmosphere so much like South Africa that it is not comfortable for an American citizen to think about.

Fortunately, students in colleges in the North have realized that the students in the South will need help, so within hours $1,000 was expedited from campuses in the North to the beleaguered students in Alabama. I think we should organize to support these students in any way it is possible to do so.

As I have said before, I do not think boycotting lunch counters that are segregated in the North has much value except in letting off our own steam. But I do think that refusing to buy South African goods such as lobster tails, diamonds, caracul coats, etc., none of which we buy every day—and at the same time refusing to buy anything at all from chain stores that have segregation of any kind in our South will have a very salutary effect.

It is curious that the United States and South Africa have much the same problem. However, the degree, thank heavens, is different. But we must move forward here at home or we cannot protest with sincerity what goes on abroad.

Civil Rights Bill

NEW YORK, APRIL 11, 1960—It is a good thing that the Senate has finally passed the civil rights bill after an eight-week fight, with 42 Democrats and 29 Republicans in favor. This is only the second civil rights legislation to pass the Senate since the Reconstruction Era. The first civil rights act of 1957 was also a voting rights measure. Already those who want a really fair bill giving the Negroes their full rights are denouncing this bill, and I am quite sure that it will continue to be denounced. But I hope that it is at least a step in the right direction.

All of us in the Democratic Party, I think, owe Senator Johnson a vote of thanks. He has risked repercussions among his Southern colleagues and among his own constituents. He has made it possible for the Democrats to claim equal, if not more, responsibility for the passage of the bill, which of course should never have had to be passed for the right to vote should be something which every citizen of this country enjoys without any question. Since it was necessary to pass the bill, however, we are fortunate to have had a parliamentary leader with the skill of Senator Johnson.

My one fear is of intimidation, which I feel sure will be tried to prevent Negro citizens in the South from registering and voting. I hope the Attorney General can find ways of protecting the registration and of preventing retaliation when the Negro citizens of the South exercise their constitutional right.

It is notable that the House of Commons in London unanimously approved the resolution deploring South Africa's racial policies and urging the British government to voice a strong feeling of disapproval at the forthcoming Commonwealth conference. It is difficult to imagine the kind of atmosphere that will exist at this conference—with Ghana, India and Great Britain itself, as well as other Commonwealth countries, protesting the policy of one of their members.

Things seem to go from bad to worse in South Africa, and nothing seems to move the people there but fear. When you have to arrest hundreds of Africans and formally ban two African political groups, you are not living in a safe community or one that has reached a point of understanding where reasonable living conditions can be arranged between the races. It is a very sad situation and one where the fundamental rights of human beings are so clearly involved that world public opinion is turning completely against South Africa.

First Lady

NEW YORK, OCTOBER 21, 1960—As we watch the Presidential campaign unroll, I wonder how many have noticed one rather interesting change in the modern type of campaign. This was brought to my attention the other day when a young newspaper reporter said to me: "Do you really think that the decision as to a man's fitness for the office of President should depend, in part at least, on what kind of a President's wife his wife will be?"

I looked at her in surprise for a moment, because it had not dawned on me what changes had come about since Mr. Eisenhower's first campaign.

Apparently we have started on a new trend. I can't remember in my husband's campaign, nor in Mr. Truman's, that such a question could be asked. Some of the children or I would accompany my husband on the various campaign trips, and if we were around at railroad stops he would introduce us to the crowd in a rather casual manner. He often said "My little boy, Jimmy," when Jimmy was as tall as he was!

My husband insisted always that a man stood on his own record. He did not bring his family in to be responsible in getting him votes or in taking the blame for his decisions. I think he sometimes found it amusing to let me do things just so as to find out what the reaction of the public would be. But nothing we did was ever calculated and thought out as part of the campaign in the way we feel that Mr. Nixon plans every appearance with his wife.

There must be times when the whole situation becomes practically unbearable, I would think, for the woman of the family. And I hope that we will return to the old and rather pleasanter way of looking upon White House families as people who have a right to their own lives.

The wives, of course, have certain official obligations, but they are certainly not responsible for their husband's policies. And they do not have to feel that sense of obligation at every point to uphold the ideas of the man of the family.

With so many people around a President who say "yes" to everything he says, it is fun sometimes for the family around him to say "no" just for the sake of devilment—but that should be a private family relaxation.

Space

HYDE PARK, MAY 8, 1961—Commander Alan Shepard's flight into space was exciting news. For us this is the beginning of more and more experiments until the day comes when we will know whether there is human life on the stars and what it is like, if so.

I must say, however, that this seems to me some time off. I am still more concerned with what happens to us here on earth and what we make of our life here than I am about these remarkable experiments. I know they have great value, and undoubtedly important discoveries arising from these experiments will help us here on earth. But I hope we are particularly careful not to send our man into orbit as the Russians did until we are sure that the return has been safeguarded as far as is humanly possible. The differences between our system and that of the Russians is a regard for human life, and I do not want to see us lose any of this regard.

We must congratulate astronaut Shepard—and, incidentally, his wife—for the courage and endurance in the training period leading up to this triumph. Let us hope that all those who carry forward these extraordinary achievements will come home as successfully to receive a grateful nation's acclaim.

Cold War

NEW YORK, DECEMBER 20, 1961—What can one woman do to prevent war? This is the question that comes my way in any number of letters these days.

In times past, the question usually asked by women was "How can we best help to defend our nation?" I cannot remember a time when the question on so many people's lips was "How can we prevent war?"

There is a widespread understanding among the people of this nation, and probably among the people of the world, that there is no safety except through the prevention of war. For many years war has been looked upon as almost inevitable in the solution of any question that has arisen between nations, and the nation that was strong enough to do so went about building up its defenses and its power to attack. It felt that it could count on these two things for safety.

There was a point then in increasing a nation's birth rate: Providing more soldiers. There was a point in creating new weapons: At their worst, they could not destroy the world as a whole.

Now, all a citizen can do is watch his government use its scientists to invent more powerful ways of achieving world destruction more and more quickly.

As I travel around this country I cannot help thinking what a pity it would be to destroy so much beauty, and I am sure this thought crosses the mind of many a Russian traveling through his country—in fact, the mind of anyone traveling anywhere in the world. Peoples of the world who have not yet achieved a place in the sun must feel this even more deeply than those of us who have had years of development and acquired resultant comforts and pleasures.

A consciousness of the fact that war means practically total destruction is the reason, I think, for the rising tide to prevent what seems such a senseless procedure.

I understand that it is perhaps difficult for some people, whose lives have been lived with a sense of the need for military development, to envisage the possibility of being no longer needed. But the average citizen is beginning to think more and more of the need to develop machinery to settle difficulties in the world without destruction or the use of atomic bombs.

Of course, if any war is permitted to break out, it is self-evident that the losing side would use atomic bombs if they were available. So the only thing to do is to put this atomic power into the hands of the United Nations and have it used only for peaceful purposes. Here is where the individual comes in. To the women and the men who are asking themselves "What can I do as an individual?" my answer is this: Take a more active interest in your government, have a say in who is nominated for political office, work for these candidates and keep in close touch with them if they are elected. If our objective is to do away with the causes of war, build up the United Nations and give the UN more control over the weapons of total destruction, we should urge that world law be developed so that people's grievances can be heard promptly and judiciously settled.

We should begin in our own environment and in our own community as far as possible to build a peace-loving attitude and learn to discipline ourselves to accept, in the small things of our lives, mediation and arbitration.

As individuals, there is little that any of us can do to prevent an accidental use of bombs in the hands of those who already have them. We can register, however, with our government a firm protest against granting the knowledge and the use of these weapons to those who do not now have them.

We may hope that in the years to come, when the proper machinery is set up, such lethal weapons can be destroyed wherever they are and the knowledge that developed them can be used for more constructive purposes.

In the meantime, no citizen of a democracy need feel completely helpless if he becomes an active factor in the citizenship of his community. For it is the willingness to abdicate responsibilities of citizenship which gives us our feeling of inadequacy and frustration. As long as we are not actually destroyed, we can work to gain greater understanding of other peoples and to try to present to the peoples of the world the values of our own beliefs. We can do this by demonstrating our conviction that human life is worth preserving and that we are willing to help others to enjoy benefits of our civilization just as we have enjoyed it.

Commission on the Status of Women

PARIS, FEBRUARY 16, 1962—Before coming over here my last two days in the United States were spent largely in Washington, D.C., and I want to tell about them before writing about my current month-long trip.

On last Monday morning in the White House the President opened the first meeting of the Commission on the Status of Women. After very brief preliminaries and upon being introduced by Secretary of Labor Arthur Goldberg, President Kennedy put us all at ease by starting the conference off on a note of levity by remarking that he had appointed the commission in self-defense—self-defense against an able and persistent newspaperwoman, Miss May Craig. No other lady of the press has waged a longer or more persistent battle for the rights of women than has May Craig, and I am sure she is flattered by the President's recognition of her tremendous interest in the field of women's equality.

After the morning session we had lunch in a downstairs restaurant that did not exist in my day there but which must be a tremendous convenience for those working in the White House today. A guide showed us around the White House, telling us about certain things that have been changed under Mrs. Kennedy's direction and which she explained to the American people over two television networks this week.

The basement floor and the first floor for entertaining have certainly been made far more attractive than ever before. Mrs. Kennedy has succeeded in having presented to the White House some really very beautiful pieces of furniture and decorative pictures, which add enormously to the interest of these rooms.

We kept ourselves strictly on schedule all day and opened our afternoon meeting promptly at 2 o'clock at 200 Maryland Avenue, below the Capitol, where the Commission on the Status of Women will have its permanent office.

We soon began to discuss the best way to organize to achieve the maximum of work not only on the six points laid down in the President's directive to the commission but in other situations which will certainly arise. The commission will try to make its influence felt concerning women's problems not only in the federal area but in state and local areas and in industry as well as in women's home responsibilities.

The effort, of course, is to find how we can best use the potentialities of women without impairing their first responsibilities, which are to their homes, their husbands and their children. We need to use in the very best way possible all our available manpower—and that includes womanpower—and this commission, I think, can well point out some of the ways in which this can be accomplished.

I was glad to hear brought up the question of part-time work for women and of better training in certain areas because the possibilities available to women could be more widely publicized and education could be directed to meet and prepare for these new openings.

The Vice President and Mrs. Johnson gave a delightful reception at their home in the late afternoon for the members of the commission.

The meetings continued through Tuesday morning and into early afternoon, and I felt that the discussions had brought us to a point where we could get the staff to continue with the organization and start some of our subcommittees to working very shortly.

I was back at my home in New York City by 5:30 P.M. on Tuesday and a few people came in to say goodbye at 6 o'clock and then I packed and dressed and was ready to leave the house a little after 10 o'clock. My secretary, Miss Maureen Corr, and I left by Air France for Paris at midnight and had a most delightful trip—smooth and comfortable. We are now at the Crillon Hotel, where I always feel at home because of the many months I've stayed here when we used to hold meetings of the General Assembly of the United Nations in Paris.

Henry Morgenthau III met us at Orly Airport and told us of the plans made for doing two educational television programs, and a little later we were joined at the hotel by Professor Alfred Gorsser for discussion of our joint responsibilities on the programs. By this time it was 7:00 P.M. Paris time, though only 1:00 P.M. New York time, and after a delightful dinner we felt well adjusted to the change and feel well prepared for busy days ahead.

UNIVERSAL DECLARATION OF HUMAN RIGHTS
[complete text]

Preamble

WHEREAS recognition of the inherent dignity and of the equal and inalienable rights of all members of the human family is the foundation of freedom, justice and peace in the world,

WHEREAS disregard and contempt for human rights have resulted in barbarous acts which have outraged the conscience of mankind, and the advent of a world in which human beings shall enjoy freedom of speech and belief and freedom from fear and want has been proclaimed as the highest aspiration of the common people,

WHEREAS it is essential, if man is not to be compelled to have recourse, as a last resort, to rebellion against tyranny and oppression, that human rights should be protected by the rule of law,

WHEREAS it is essential to promote the development of friendly relations between nations,

WHEREAS the peoples of the United Nations have in the Charter reaffirmed their faith in fundamental human rights, in the dignity and worth of the human person and in the equal rights of men and women and have determined to promote social progress and better standards of life in larger freedom,

WHEREAS Member States have pledged themselves to achieve, in co-operation with the United Nations, the promotion of universal respect for and observance of human rights and fundamental freedoms,

WHEREAS a common understanding of these rights and freedoms is of the greatest importance for the full realization of this pledge,

Now, Therefore, THE GENERAL ASSEMBLY Proclaims

THIS UNIVERSAL DECLARATION OF HUMAN RIGHTS as a common standard of achievement for all peoples and all nations, to the end that every individual and every organ of society, keeping this Declaration constantly in mind, shall strive by teaching and education to promote respect for these rights and freedoms and by progressive measures, national and international, to secure their universal and effective recognition and observance, both among the peoples of Member States themselves and among the peoples of territories under their jurisdiction.

Article 1.

All human beings are born free and equal in dignity and rights. They are endowed with reason and conscience and should act towards one another in a spirit of brotherhood.

Article 2.

Everyone is entitled to all the rights and freedoms set forth in this Declaration, without distinction of any kind, such as race, color, sex, language, religion, political or other opinion, national or social origin, property, birth or other status. Furthermore, no distinction shall be made on the basis of the political, jurisdictional or international status of the country or territory to which a person belongs, whether it be independent, trust, non–self-governing or under any other limitation of sovereignty.

Article 3.

Everyone has the right to life, liberty and security of person.

Article 4.

No one shall be held in slavery or servitude; slavery and the slave trade shall be prohibited in all their forms.

Article 5.

No one shall be subjected to torture or to cruel, inhuman or degrading treatment or punishment.

Article 6.

Everyone has the right to recognition everywhere as a person before the law.

Article 7.

All are equal before the law and are entitled without any discrimination to equal protection of the law. All are entitled to equal protection against any discrimination in violation of this Declaration and against any incitement to such discrimination.

Article 8.

Everyone has the right to an effective remedy by the competent national tribunals for acts violating the fundamental rights granted him by the constitution or by law.

Article 9.

No one shall be subjected to arbitrary arrest, detention or exile.

Article 10.

Everyone is entitled in full equality to a fair and public hearing by an independent and impartial tribunal, in the determination of his rights and obligations and of any criminal charge against him.

Article 11.

(1) Everyone charged with a penal offence has the right to be presumed innocent until proved guilty according to law in a public trial at which he has had all the guarantees necessary for his defense.

(2) No one shall be held guilty of any penal offence on account of any act or omission which did not constitute a penal offence, under national or international law, at the time when it was committed. Nor shall a heavier penalty be imposed than the one that was applicable at the time the penal offence was committed.

Article 12.

No one shall be subjected to arbitrary interference with his privacy, family, home or correspondence, nor to attacks upon his honor and reputation. Everyone has the right to the protection of the law against such interference or attacks.

Article 13.

(1) Everyone has the right to freedom of movement and residence within the borders of each state.

(2) Everyone has the right to leave any country, including his own, and to return to his country.

Article 14.

(1) Everyone has the right to seek and to enjoy in other countries asylum from persecution.

(2) This right may not be invoked in the case of prosecutions genuinely arising from non-political crimes or from acts contrary to the purposes and principles of the United Nations.

Article 15.

(1) Everyone has the right to a nationality.

(2) No one shall be arbitrarily deprived of his nationality nor denied the right to change his nationality.

Article 16.

(1) Men and women of full age, without any limitation due to race, nationality or religion, have the right to marry and

to found a family. They are entitled to equal rights as to marriage, during marriage and at its dissolution.

(2) Marriage shall be entered into only with the free and full consent of the intending spouses.

(3) The family is the natural and fundamental group unit of society and is entitled to protection by society and the State.

Article 17.

(1) Everyone has the right to own property alone as well as in association with others.

(2) No one shall be arbitrarily deprived of his property.

Article 18.

Everyone has the right to freedom of thought, conscience and religion; this right includes freedom to change his religion or belief, and freedom, either alone or in community with others and in public or private, to manifest his religion or belief in teaching, practice, worship and observance.

Article 19.

Everyone has the right to freedom of opinion and expression; this right includes freedom to hold opinions without interference and to seek, receive and impart information and ideas through any media and regardless of frontiers.

Article 20.

(1) Everyone has the right to freedom of peaceful assembly and association.

(2) No one may be compelled to belong to an association.

Article 21.

(1) Everyone has the right to take part in the government of his country, directly or through freely chosen representatives.

(2) Everyone has the right to equal access to public service in his country.

(3) The will of the people shall be the basis of the authority of government; this shall be expressed in periodic and genuine elections which shall be by universal and equal suffrage and shall be held by secret vote or by equivalent free voting procedures.

Article 22.

Everyone, as a member of society, has the right to social security and is entitled to realization, through national effort and international co-operation and in accordance with the organization and resources of each State, of the economic, social and cultural rights indispensable for his dignity and the free development of his personality.

Article 23.

(1) Everyone has the right to work, to free choice of employment, to just and favorable conditions of work and to protection against unemployment.

(2) Everyone, without any discrimination, has the right to equal pay for equal work.

(3) Everyone who works has the right to just and favorable remuneration ensuring for himself and his family an existence worthy of human dignity, and supplemented, if necessary, by other means of social protection.

(4) Everyone has the right to form and to join trade unions for the protection of his interests.

Article 24.

Everyone has the right to rest and leisure, including reasonable limitation of working hours and periodic holidays with pay.

Article 25.

(1) Everyone has the right to a standard of living adequate for the health and well-being of himself and of his family, including food, clothing, housing and medical care and necessary social services, and the right to security in the event of unemployment, sickness, disability, widowhood, old age or other lack of livelihood in circumstances beyond his control.

(2) Motherhood and childhood are entitled to special care and assistance. All children, whether born in or out of wedlock, shall enjoy the same social protection.

Article 26.

(1) Everyone has the right to education. Education shall be free, at least in the elementary and fundamental stages. Elementary education shall be compulsory. Technical and professional education shall be made generally available and higher education shall be equally accessible to all on the basis of merit.

(2) Education shall be directed to the full development of the human personality and to the strengthening of respect for human rights and fundamental freedoms. It shall promote understanding, tolerance and friendship among all na-

tions, racial or religious groups, and shall further the activities of the United Nations for the maintenance of peace.

(3) Parents have a prior right to choose the kind of education that shall be given to their children.

Article 27.

(1) Everyone has the right freely to participate in the cultural life of the community, to enjoy the arts and to share in scientific advancement and its benefits.

(2) Everyone has the right to the protection of the moral and material interests resulting from any scientific, literary or artistic production of which he is the author.

Article 28.

Everyone is entitled to a social and international order in which the rights and freedoms set forth in this Declaration can be fully realized.

Article 29.

(1) Everyone has duties to the community in which alone the free and full development of his personality is possible.

(2) In the exercise of his rights and freedoms, everyone shall be subject only to such limitations as are determined by law solely for the purpose of securing due recognition and respect for the rights and freedoms of others and of meeting the just requirements of morality, public order and the general welfare in a democratic society.

(3) These rights and freedoms may in no case be exercised contrary to the purposes and principles of the United Nations.

Article 30.

Nothing in this Declaration may be interpreted as implying for any State, group or person any right to engage in any activity or to perform any act aimed at the destruction of any of the rights and freedoms set forth herein.

ELEANOR ROOSEVELT'S OBITUARY

The New York Times
Thursday, November 8, 1962 (Excerpts)

MRS. ROOSEVELT DIES AT 78
AFTER ILLNESS OF SIX WEEKS

Mrs. Franklin D. Roosevelt died last night.

The former First Lady, famous as the wife and widow of the 32d President of the United States and an international figure in her own right, died at 6:15 P.M. in her home at East 74th Street. She was 78 years old.

Reaction to Mrs. Roosevelt's death was quick and deep.

The woman who was a noted humanitarian, author and columnist, delegate to the United Nations and active force in the Democratic party was mourned by people over the world. President Kennedy called her "one of the great ladies in the history of this country." The President and former President Harry S. Truman announced they planned to attend Mrs. Roosevelt's funeral.

Mrs. Franklin D. Roosevelt was more involved in the minds and hearts and aspirations of people than any other First Lady in history. By the end of her life she was one of the most esteemed women in the world.

During her 12 years in the White House she was sometimes laughed at and sometimes bitterly resented. But during her last years she became the object of almost universal respect.

Again and again, she was voted "the world's most admired woman" in international polls. When she entered the halls of the United Nations, representatives from all countries rose to honor her. She had become not only the wife and widow of a towering President but a noble personality in herself.

In the White House and for some time thereafter, no First Lady could touch Mrs. Roosevelt for causes espoused, opinions expressed, distances spanned, people spoken to, words printed, precedents shattered, honors conferred, degrees garnered. She was as indigenous to America as palms to a Florida coastline, and as the nation's most peripatetic woman, she brought her warmth, sincerity, zeal and patience to every corner of the land and to much of the world.

Her seemingly ceaseless activity and energy provoked both a kind of dazzled admiration and numberless "Eleanor" jokes, particularly in the nineteen thirties and forties. The derision fell away at the end; the admiration deepened.

Held in High Esteem

After her husband's death and a career as mistress of the White House that shattered precedents with a regularity never approached by Abigail Adams and Dolley Madison, President Harry S. Truman appointed Mrs. Roosevelt in 1945 a delegate to the General Assembly.

The esteem in which Mrs. Roosevelt was held in this country was immense, despite intense criticism that some observers held stemmed from persons who differed politically and ideologically with her husband. She was accused of stimulating racial prejudices, of meddling in politics, talking too much, being too informal and espousing causes critics felt a mistress of the White House should have left alone. She even became what she called a "phony issue" in her husband's campaigns for re-election.

On the other hand, she was hailed by countless numbers as their personal champion in a world first depression-ridden, then war-torn and finally maladjusted in the postwar years. She was a symbol of the new role women were to play in the world. As a result of her work in the United Nations, particularly in behalf of the little peoples of the world, this esteem soon transcended national barriers to become virtually worldwide.

Although she was no longer First Lady, her influences had diminished but little. A typical example of the kind of enthusiasm she could arouse abroad, one among many examples, occurred during Mrs. Roosevelt's visit to Luxembourg in 1950. Perle Mesta was then American Minister to that country.

One of Mrs. Roosevelt's first acts was to call upon the Grand Duchess in her palace—a long call. To catch just a glimpse of her, thousands of Luxembourgers stood outside for hours in an unrelenting rain, calling again and again: "Mees-ees Roose-velt! Mees-ees Roose-velt!"

Thousands more turned out later throughout the tiny country in villages gay with banners and flowers and smiling faces. In her distinctive warbling falsetto, she thanked as many as she could.

Mrs. Roosevelt was an enthusiastic airplane traveler. She went down into the mines. She wandered throughout the world with little ostentation. She maintained a prodigious correspondence.

Her Influence Questioned

The more important chroniclers of Mrs. Roosevelt's day in the White House have noted few instances in which it could be established that her counsels were of first importance in changing the tide of affairs. Nor did President Roosevelt always confide in his wife where matters of state were concerned. For example, he did not tell her that he was going to Newfoundland to confer with Prime Minister Winston Churchill of Britain on matters concerning the war. He merely told her that he was "going on a trip through the Cape Cod Canal."

There were, however, many known incidents in which Mrs. Roosevelt was able to direct the President's attention to such matters as injustices done to racial or religious minorities in the armed services or elsewhere in the Government.

With characteristic feminine candor, Mrs. Roosevelt always insisted that she had to do what she felt was right. As a result, injustice and inequality, whether manifested by such diverse agencies as the State Department or the Russians, evoked a strong reaction. Mrs. Roosevelt got along well with the State Department until the Palestine issue arose. In February and March of 1948 she publicly opposed American policy, which maintained an arms embargo on shipment of arms to Israelis. She also came out in favor of partitioning Palestine into Jewish and Arab states.

While often critical of Soviet tactics, Mrs. Roosevelt consistently urged the United States to continue efforts to end the cold war by negotiation. She also advocated the abandonment of nuclear weapons tests and called for United States recognition of Red China.

Some of the most serious criticism leveled at Mrs. Roosevelt followed her support and sponsorship of a number of groups in which Communists and "fellow-travelers" were active. She often pointed out that she recognized a person's right to be a Communist, provided he did not deny this affiliation. Later, however, she pointed out that experience had taught her that it was impossible to work with Communist dominated groups. In 1949, Mrs. Roosevelt became embroiled in a bitter controversy with Cardinal Spellman, Roman Catholic Archbishop of New York. It followed some remarks she had made against use of federal funds for parochial schools.

In discussing a measure for aid to education then before Congress, Mrs. Roosevelt wrote in her "My Day" column that "those of us who believe in the right of any human being to belong to whatever church he sees fit, and to worship God in his own way, cannot be accused of prejudice when we do not want to see public education connected with religious control of the schools, which are paid for by taxpayers' money." The Cardinal accused Mrs. Roosevelt of ignorance and prejudice and called her columns "documents of discrimination unworthy of an American mother."

The dispute was ultimately resolved amicably, but not before it was waged by leading members of the clergy and became an issue in the 1949 campaign as political figures aligned themselves for and against Mrs. Roosevelt. It ended in August of that year when Cardinal Spellman called on Mrs. Roosevelt at her Hyde Park home and both issued statements clarifying what they said had been a "misunderstanding."

Her service as a delegate to the United Nations began under President Truman in 1947 and ended, temporarily, in 1952. In 1961, President Kennedy appointed her as one of five members of the United States delegation to the 15th session of the General Assembly. In the intervening years, Mrs. Roosevelt devoted herself to her syndicated newspaper column and to the American Association for the United Nations. When leading Democrats formed the National Issues Committee in an effort to restore Democratic control of the Federal Government, she accepted its national chairmanship.

Mrs. Roosevelt never lost interest in the Democratic party. She addressed its national convention in 1952 and 1956, and both years campaigned for Adlai E. Stevenson. At the 1960 convention in Los Angeles, she pressed for a Stevenson-Kennedy ticket and seconded Mr. Stevenson's nomination.

Throughout her years of association with the party, Mrs. Roosevelt had been identified with its liberal wing. In 1959, speaking at a dinner in honor of her 75th birthday, she took sharp issue with former President Truman, who also addressed the dinner. Mr. Truman lashed out at "hothouse liberals" whom he accused of hurting the cause of liberalism and inviting the way for reaction. Mrs. Roosevelt replied, saying: "I know we need a united party. But it cannot be a united party that gives up its principles."

The same year she joined with former Senator Herbert H. Lehman in a drive to consolidate the Democratic reform movement in New York City to oust Carmine G. DeSapio, leader of Tammany Hall.

The next year she again aligned herself with the reform group and stumped for Senator John F. Kennedy. Her most recent political activity was as leader, with Mr. Lehman, of the reform faction during the 1961 mayoralty race in New York and during the 1962 primaries. Her candidate in 1961, Mayor Wagner, won re-election by more than 400,000 votes.

Theodore Roosevelt's Niece

Anna Eleanor Roosevelt was born to Elliott and Anna Hall Roosevelt in New York on Oct. 11, 1884. Theodore Roosevelt, the 25th President, was her uncle. The families of both her parents were prominent socially, the Roosevelts a wealthy family of Dutch descent and the Halls of the same family as Philip Livingston, the English descended signer of the Declaration of Independence.

Mrs. Roosevelt's father was known as a sportsman and big game hunter, and her mother was a noted beauty of the day. When Eleanor was 8 her mother died, and the young girl went to live with her maternal grandmother, Mrs. Valentine G. Hall, at Tivoli, N.Y., not far from Poughkeepsie. Her father died a year and a half later.

She was taught at home by tutors for the most part, and she recalled later in her autobiography, *This Is My Story*, that her real education did not begin until she went abroad at the age of 15.

As a child she worried because her mother and other members of her family were somewhat disappointed in young

Eleanor's appearance. When she was 15 the family decided that it would be better to supplement her social chances by a finishing trip abroad. In 1899 she was taken to England and placed in Allenswood, a school conducted by a Miss Souvestre, whom her grandmother remembered as a stimulating and cultured lady who had instructed her in her own youth.

She remained abroad for three years, studying languages, literature and history under Miss Souvestre, perfecting her French and Italian, and spending her vacations traveling on the Continent and absorbing European culture. She was drilled in the French system of acquiring and repeating precise judgment on everything.

At the age of 18 she was brought back to New York for her debut. "It was simply awful," she said in a public discussion once. "It was a beautiful party, of course, but I was so unhappy, because a girl who comes out is so utterly miserable if she does not know all the young people. Of course I had been so long abroad that I had lost touch with all the girls I used to know in New York. I was miserable through all that."

She was relieved of her misery within two years by meeting Franklin Delano Roosevelt, who had graduated from Harvard in 1904 and had come to New York to attend the Columbia Law School. He was serious-minded and intent on a career. He found Miss Roosevelt good company.

Besides the two Roosevelts were distant cousins; they had met first when he was 4 years old and she 2; and they got along easily together. Their relatives approved so highly that the marriage followed naturally. President Roosevelt came from the White House to New York on March 17, 1905, to give the bride in marriage.

After the wedding, a brilliant social event in New York, Mrs. Roosevelt passed into domesticity and maternity for a score of years. The couple's first child, Allan, was born in 1906. Eighteen months later a son, James, was born. A second son named Franklin D. Jr. died three months after birth. Three more sons, Elliott, another Franklin D. Jr., and John Aspinwall, were born during the first 11 years of marriage.

Mrs. Roosevelt had her first brush with politics and government in 1911 after Mr. Roosevelt had been elected a State Senator and the family moved to Albany. In 1913 the Roosevelts went to Washington when the future President was appointed Assistant Secretary of the Navy in the Wilson Administration. In 1920 she saw more of the political scene when her husband was a candidate for the Vice Presidency on the Democratic ticket with James M. Cox, who ran for President against Warren G. Harding. The next year poliomyelitis struck her husband, and Mrs. Roosevelt attended him and encouraged him for three years until it was evident that any further recovery would come slowly through the remainder of his life.

It was at this point that Mrs. Roosevelt emerged seriously in search of a career. Friends of the family and Mr. Roosevelt's physicians urged Mrs. Roosevelt to work with her husband in an effort to rekindle his interests. Some observers felt that shortly thereafter her determined introduction of activity after activity into her own life and his was a deliberate maneuver to rescue him from his invalidism, and force him to resume his former interest in affairs of the outside world.

A READER'S GUIDE

Selected Books About Franklin and Eleanor Roosevelt

Books primarily about FDR, but with references also to Mrs. Roosevelt, are noted (*). Otherwise, works are mainly about Mrs. Roosevelt. Most of these are listed also by the Franklin D. Roosevelt Presidential Library and Museum.

Where appropriate, the grade-school reading level is indicated as judged by educators or publishers.

Asbell, Bernard. *Mother and Daughter: The Letters of Eleanor and Anna Roosevelt*. Fromm, 1988.

Ayres, Alex, ed. *The Wit and Wisdom of Eleanor Roosevelt*. Meridian, 1966.

Beasley, Maurine H. *Eleanor Roosevelt and the Media: A Public Quest for Self-Fulfillment*. University of Illinois Press, 1987.

Berger, Jason. *A New Deal for the World: Eleanor Roosevelt and American Foreign Policy*. Social Science Monographs. Distributed by Columbia University Press, 1981.

Black, Allida M. *Casting Her Own Shadow: Eleanor Roosevelt and the Shaping of Postwar Liberalism*. Columbia University Press, 1996.

Black, Allida M., ed. *Courage in a Dangerous World : The Political Writings of Eleanor Roosevelt*. Columbia University Press,

1999. A comprehensive bibliography of magazine articles by Mrs. Roosevelt is included in this work.

Black, Ruby. *Eleanor Roosevelt. A Biography.* Duell, Sloan and Pearce, 1940.

Blassingame, Wyatt. *Eleanor Roosevelt.* Putnam, 1967. (Grades 2–4)

Burns, James M. *Roosevelt: The Lion and the Fox.* Harcourt, Brace, Jovanovich, 1956.*

———. *Roosevelt: The Soldier of Freedom.* Harcourt, Brace, Jovanovich, 1970.*

Butturff, Dorothy Dow. *Eleanor Roosevelt, An Eager Spirit: The Letters of Dorothy Dow, 1933–45.* Ed. Ruth K. McClure. Norton, 1984.

Chadakoff, Rochelle, ed. *Eleanor Roosevelt's My Day: Vol. I, Her Acclaimed Columns, 1936–1945.* Pharos Books, 1989.

Cook, Blanche Wiesen. *Eleanor Roosevelt: Volume One, 1884–1933.* Viking, 1992.

Curtis, Sandra R. *Alice and Eleanor, A Contrast in Style and Purpose.* Bowling Green State University, 1994.

David, Kenneth S. *F.D.R.: The Beckoning of Destiny, 1882–1928.* Putnam, 1973.*

Davidson, Margaret. *The Story of Eleanor Roosevelt.* Scholastic, 1968. (Grades 7 and up)

Douglas, Helen Gahagan. *The Eleanor Roosevelt We Remember.* Hill & Wang, 1963.

Eaton, Jeannette. *The Story of Eleanor Roosevelt.* Morrow, 1956. (Grades 7 and up)

Emblidge, David, ed. *Eleanor Roosevelt's My Day, Vol. II: The Post-war Years, 1945–1952. Her Acclaimed Columns.* Pharos, 1990.

————. *Eleanor Roosevelt's My Day, Vol. III: First Lady of the World. Her Acclaimed Columns 1953–1962.* Pharos, 1991.

Flemion, Jess, and Colleen O'Connor, eds. *Eleanor Roosevelt: An American Journey.* San Diego State University Press, 1987.

Freedman, Russell. *Eleanor Roosevelt: A Life of Discovery.* Clarion, 1993.

Galbraith, John Kenneth. *A Life in Our Times.* Houghton, Mifflin, 1981.

Goodwin, Doris Kearns. *No Ordinary Time: Franklin and Eleanor Roosevelt: The Home Front in World War II.* Simon & Schuster, 1994.

Graves, Charles. *Eleanor Roosevelt: First Lady of the World.* Garrard, 1966. (Grades 2–4).

Gurewitsch, A. David. *Eleanor Roosevelt: Her Day; A Personal Album.* Quadrangle, 1974.

Hareven, Tamara K. *Eleanor Roosevelt: An American Conscience.* Quadrangle, 1968.

Harrity, Richard, and Ralph Martin. *Eleanor Roosevelt: Her Life in Pictures*. Duell, Sloan and Pearce, 1958.

Hershan, Stella K. *A Woman of Quality*. Crown, 1970.

———. *The Candles She Lit: The Legacy of Eleanor Roosevelt*. Praeger, 1993.

Hickok, Lorena A. *Eleanor Roosevelt: Reluctant First Lady*. Dodd, Mead, 1980.

———. *The Story of Eleanor Roosevelt*. Grosset and Dunlap, 1959. (Grades 7–9)

Hoff-Wilson, Joan, and Marjorie Lightman, eds. *Without Precedent: The Life and Career of Eleanor Roosevelt*. Indiana University Press, 1984.

Jacobs, William Jay. *Eleanor Roosevelt: A Life of Happiness and Tears*. Coward-McCann, 1983.

Johnson, George. *Eleanor Roosevelt: The Compelling Life Story of One of the Most Famous Women of Our Time*. Monarch Books, 1962.

Kearney, James. *Anna Eleanor Roosevelt: The Evolution of a Reformer*. Houghton, Mifflin, 1968.

Knapp, Sally E. *Eleanor Roosevelt, A Biography*. Crowell, 1949. (Grade 7 and up)

Larabee, Eric. *Commander in Chief*. Harper & Row, 1987.*

Lash, Joseph P. *Eleanor Roosevelt: A Friend's Memoir*. Doubleday, 1964.

————. *A World of Love: Eleanor Roosevelt and Her Friends, 1943–1962.* Doubleday, 1984.

————. *Eleanor and Franklin: The Story of Their Relationship, Based on Eleanor Roosevelt's Private Papers.* Norton, 1971.

————. *Life Was Meant to Be Lived: A Contemporary Portrait of Eleanor Roosevelt.* Norton, 1984.

————. *Love, Eleanor: Eleanor Roosevelt and Her Friends.* Doubleday, 1982.

————. *Eleanor: The Years Alone.* Norton, 1972.

Leuchtenburg, William. *Franklin D. Roosevelt and the New Deal.* Harper & Row, 1963.*

MacLeish, Archibald. *The Eleanor Roosevelt Story.* Houghton, Mifflin, 1965.

McKown, Robin. *Eleanor Roosevelt's World.* Grosset and Dunlap, 1964. (Grade 7 and up)

Miller, Nathan. *F.D.R.: An Intimate Biography.* Doubleday, 1983.*

Oursler, Fulton. *Behold This Dreamer!* Little, Brown, 1964.

Perkins, Frances. *The Roosevelt I Knew.* Viking Press, 1946.*

Roosevelt, David B. *Grandmére: A Personal History of Eleanor Roosevelt.* Warner Books, 2002.

Roosevelt, Elliott. *Eleanor Roosevelt, With Love: A Centenary Remembrance.* Dutton, 1984.

————. *An Untold Story: The Roosevelts of Hyde Park.* Putnam, 1973.

Roosevelt, Elliott, and James Brough. *Mother R: Eleanor Roosevelt's Untold Story.* Putnam, 1977.

Roosevelt, James, and Bill Libby. *My Parents: A Different View.* Playboy Press, 1976.

Scharf, Lois. *ER: First Lady of American Liberalism.* Twayne, 1987.

Somerville, Mollie D. *Eleanor Roosevelt As I Knew Her.* EPM Publications, 1996.

Steinberg, Alfred. *Mrs. R: The Life of Eleanor Roosevelt.* Putnam, 1958. See also 1959 edition. (Grades 2–5)

Streitmatter, Rodger, ed. *Empty Without You: The Intimate Letters of Eleanor Roosevelt and Lorena Hickok.* Free Press, 1998.

Ward, Geoffrey C. *Before the Trumpet: Young Franklin Roosevelt. 1882–1905.* Harper & Row, 1985.*

————. *A First Class Temperament: The Emergence of Frankin E. Roosevelt (1905–1928).* Harper & Row. 1989.*

Watrous, Hilda R. *In League with Eleanor: Eleanor Roosevelt and the League of Women Voters, 1921–1962.* Foundation for Citizenship Education, League of Women Voters, 1984.

Weil, Ann. *Eleanor Roosevelt. Courageous Girl.* Bobbs, Merrill, 1965. (Grade 2–5).

Whitney, Sharon. *Eleanor Roosevelt*. F. Watts, 1982. (Grade 7 and up)

Woolley, A. E., ed. *Expressions: Eleanor on Her Life*. Woolley Publications, 1984.

Youngs, William J. *Eleanor Roosevelt: A Personal and Political Life*. Little, Brown, 1985.

Books by Eleanor Roosevelt

When You Grow Up to Vote. Houghton, Mifflin, 1932.

It's Up to the Women. Stokes, 1933.

This Is My Story. Harper, 1937.

My Days. Dodge, 1938.

This Troubled World. Kinsey, 1938.

Christmas. A.A. Knopf, 1940.

Roosevelt, Eleanor, and Frances Cooke MacGregor. *This Is America*. Putnam, 1942.

If You Ask Me. Appleton-Century, 1946.

Personal Recollections, Franklin D. Roosevelt and Hyde Park. 1949.

This I Remember. Harper, 1949.

Roosevelt, Eleanor, and Helen Ferris. *Partners: The United Nations and Youth*. Doubleday, 1950.

India and the Awakening East. Harper, 1953.

Roosevelt, Eleanor, and William Dewitt. *UN: Today and Tomorrow*. Harper, 1953.

It Seems to Me. Norton, 1954.

Roosevelt, Eleanor, and Lorena Hickok. *Ladies of Courage*. Putnam, 1954.

On My Own. Harper, 1958.

Tor, Regina, and Eleanor Roosevelt. *Growing Toward Peace*. Random House, 1960.

You Learn by Living. Harper, 1960.

The Autobiography of Eleanor Roosevelt. Harper, 1961.

Roosevelt, Eleanor, and Helen Ferris. *Your Teens and Mine*. Doubleday, 1961. (Grade 7 and up)

Eleanor Roosevelt's Book of Common Sense Etiquette. Macmillan, 1962.

The Wisdom of Eleanor Roosevelt: Eleanor Roosevelt Writes About Her World. McCall Corp., 1962.

Eleanor Roosevelt's Christmas Book. Dodd, Mead, 1963.

Tomorrow Is Now. Harper & Row, 1963.

The Autobiography of Eleanor Roosevelt. Da Capo Press, 1992.

What I Hope to Leave Behind: The Essential Essays of Eleanor Roosevelt. Allida M. Black, ed. Carlson, 1995.

INDEX TO QUOTATIONS

Numbers in this index refer to quotations, not pages unless preceded by the letter "p."

Concepts as well as selected words from the quotations of this book are indexed here. Also indexed, by date, are titles of the selected "My Day" articles in the appendix.

A selection of Mrs. Roosevelt's key themes as seen in this collection of quotations are set in **boldface**.

rumors of, 154
Russians and, 152
stopping, 15
war, future, 40
warning citizens at bomb
sites, 266
Washington experience, 173
watchfulness, 45
weakness that goes wrong,
280
wealth, flaunting, 229
real, 258
weapon, outlawed, 253
weariness, 368
White House years, 173, 189
wife, as hostess and guest,
382
winning, suffering and, 48,
55
wisdom, 126, 132, 155, 332
and survival, 131
mistakes and, 87
use of, 131
women
adjustment by, 370
anxiety and, 188
appreciation of, 305
are not all alike, 83
communication by, 263
courage of, 193
deepest satisfaction of,
371
future respect for, 39
in office, 82

influence of, 252
interests of, 81
judging work of, 84
kinds of, 85
peace and, 43, 44
politics and, 54, 81, 82
self-trained, 61
supporting, 84
types of, 257
understanding, 37
uniting interests of, 85
war and, 193
work of, 136
working, 39
"Women and
Employment," **My
Day,** July 13, 1939, p. 101
"Women and Population,"
My Day, May 13, 1955,
p. 128
"Women and Work," **My
Day,** August 5, 1939,
p. 105
"Women in War," **My Day,**
October 15, 1943, p. 114
words, unnecessary, 205
work, 10
basic right to, 59
completing, 286
conviction and, 128
interesting, 46
permanence of good, 97
satisfaction of, 166
to repay, 166

ABOUT DONALD WIGAL

Donald Wigal, Ph.D., received the Distinguished Alumnus Award from the University of Dayton in 1985. He has permanent teaching certification from the City University of New York and certification from the Institute for Spiritual Theology. His liturgical theology degree is from Notre Dame. He was the indexer of the *New York Times Encyclopedia of Film,* an indexer of *Academic American Encyclopedia,* and contributor of articles to several books, including the *Encyclopedia of Mysticism and Paranormal Experience.* His most recent book is *Historical Maritime Maps Used in Exploration, 1200–1600.* Previous works include *The Visions of Nostradamus and Other Prophets.* He is a member of American Society of Composers, Authors and Publishers. He lives in New York City.